Loving Life in a Life Plan Community

Information and Stories to Help You
Find Happiness in Retirement

by Janice Arrowsmith

Acknowledgements

I give boundless, loving appreciation for my husband, Don, who provided computer expertise, ideas, questions, collaboration, and many long walks together. Greg Ferguson and Scott Westcott critiqued the book proposal. Carol DeLancey offered insights into the inner workings of an LPC. My sister, Susan, wrote a valuable critique. My children, Penelope and Pamela, have forever been sources of joy and affirmation.

"Bunnies" are copyrighted by Marilyn Deatelhauser and are used with permission.

Life Plan Communities – United States
CCRCs – United States
Retirement Communities – United States
Retirees – Housing – Senior Living – United States – Lifestyle

ISBN-10 0-9760343-5-2
ISBN-13 978-0-9760343-5-3

Published in the U.S.A. 2023

Each day provides its own gifts.

– Marcus Aurelius

The adult version of "head 'n shoulders, knees 'n toes" is "wallet, glasses, keys 'n phone!"

Table of Contents

Please note: A Life Plan Community (LPC) is also called a Continuing Care Retirement Community (CCRC). Several years ago, Leading Age, a group of not-for-profit aging services providers, adopted LPC to replace CCRC. Although in practice it has been difficult to make this change, the industry has been emphatic that Communities go in that direction. This book will use Life Plan Community (LPC) throughout the text.

The word *community* has many meanings, from a gathering of a few people to the vast world itself. In this book, *community* almost always means a Life Plan Community.

I'm starting a diet on January
1st ... or 2nd ... or on a Monday.

Web Site for the Book

https://LovingLifeInALifePlanCommunity.com is a web site for this book. You will find the following:

- How to order a copy of the book.

- Six downloadable PDFs of the charts and checklists in chapters 3, 5, and 7.

- An interview with the author.

- Reviews of the book.

- A way to contact the author.

- Errata (updated when found).

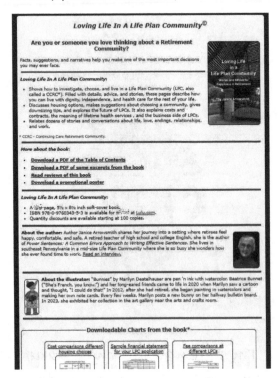

Preface

Moving to Rolling Meadow Life Plan Community[1] was no accident. Ten years before moving here, I began visiting retirement communities. I attended countless marketing events, walked many tours, enjoyed numerous brunches and lunches, asked lots of questions, collected abundant booklets, and made charts to compare them. I learned more than most people want to know!

When we were younger adults, we didn't think about becoming bent over or hard of hearing. We hoped that, if we live so long, we will remain as vibrant as we are now. Then one day, we realize that we ourselves – or perhaps our parents, relatives, or friends – are on the cusp of *old*. What do we do? Deny? Avoid? Ignore? Act?

One thing is certain: by taking charge of our own health and welfare, we give family and friends a huge gift.

This book explains why, to enjoy comfort, safety, and health care, the best place to live the rest of your life is a Life Plan Community.

Some people act without a plan. They decide too quickly, or fail to explore available options, or do not know what they really want. They may not make the best choices.

---

[1] Fictitious name for a real place.

Loving Life in a Life Plan Community explains details like thinking about the future, evaluating housing options, exploring costs, downsizing, fitting in, preserving your health, living well. Additionally, scores of residents' stories capture the camaraderie found in a Life Plan Community.

Sometimes, it's just a robe 'n
bunny-slippers kind of day.

Introduction

Having done my own detailed search for the retirement setting that would suit my husband and me, I realized that the knowledge I gained in this process could ease the path for others making this journey. I became passionate about transcribing over fifty stories that residents told of large and small incidents from their lives. Then, researching Life Plan Communities (LPCs), I discovered facts and trends that would have enriched my quest that led to this lovely retirement setting which I am calling *Rolling Meadow Life Plan Community.*

According to the Census Bureau, the population of the United States will soon contain more senior citizens than children: "By 2030, all baby boomers will be older than age sixty-five."[2] Providing for seniors' burgeoning needs for housing, personal care, and skilled nursing care is already a booming market (excuse the pun) that will continue to expand for decades to come. In huge numbers, middle-class retirees are funding lifestyles of comfort and convenience. Their top priority is also the thesis of this book: "Where can I enjoy my final years so that I will be as happy, safe, and healthy as possible?"

---

[2] "Older People Projected to Outnumber Children for First Time in U.S. History," United States Census Bureau, release number CB18-41, March 13, 2018.

Introduction

A high school guidance counselor once told me that the students best prepared to apply to college are the ones who did all their campus visits in their junior years. That way, they enter their senior year knowing where they will apply, which school is their first choice, and whom they will ask for letters of recommendation. These students are easily managing what for others can be a daunting task, and thus they enjoy to the fullest their last year of high school.

So too, the senior citizens who intend to make the transition to living in an LPC are well prepared for a healthy, happy experience if they start planning years before they make the move. When they examine their values and needs for the next twenty to forty years, they may realize that they can live their most secure, active, stimulating, sociable, and healthy lives in a Life Plan Community (LPC)[3].

Finding the LPC that matches their lifestyle and goals is important. As in their youth, seniors ask themselves, "Who am I? What do I want? How can I get it?" Exploring these questions helps them find the setting where they will thrive.

Based on my own thinking, experience, and research, I have written *Loving Life in a Life Plan Community* to show that, for many seniors, the best place to live is a Life Plan Community. An LPC provides, in one setting, three elements important for longevity and happiness – comfort, safety, and health care.

Reading *Loving Your Life in a Life Plan Community*, you sense the camaraderie that bolsters daily life in an LPC. Along the way, you share my husband's and my journey of exploring, visiting, choosing, and moving into an LPC that perfectly suits our lifestyles and goals.

---

[3] Also known as Continuing Care Retirement Communities, some communities have been renaming themselves as Life Plan Communities because senior citizens, enjoying better health and longevity than ever before, prefer to focus on *life*, not *care*.

Introduction

You learn about housing options for seniors and the advantages of living in an LPC compared to staying in the family home or moving to an over-55 development or another residential setting. In this book, you receive a clear explanation of financial details, including types of contracts, fees, and the pros and cons of owning Long Term Care insurance. By exploring behind-the-scenes elements of an LPC as a business enterprise, you become a savvy buyer.

Loving Life in a Life Plan Community balances information with narrative. I share my own experiences and insights and give you straightforward advice, all amid abundant facts, examples, and stories. My inside information is designed to tell you what you need to know about choosing and living in a Life Plan Community.

All names are fictitious, but the stories are real.

This journey will create your own insights about what counts most as we age: being safe, happy, and comfortable among people we like.

I hate it when I mean to buy
seedless grapes but instead, I
accidentally get Oreos.

1: Dignity, Choice, Independence

Questions: When should I start thinking about where to spend the rest of my life? What questions should I ask? Without having to move again, where can I live in a setting of comfort and safety, and receive care for health problems that may happen? How can a Life Plan Community extend my life?

The Time to Begin Is Now

We read about retirement in books, articles, magazines, and websites.

We visit senior citizen centers, attend hospital presentations, and interview home health agency representatives.

We hear presentations at churches, synagogues, temples, mosques, and senior centers, and we share ideas with friends and relatives.

We imagine the future: As I age and become less fit, where will I want to live? In a house? An apartment? With my children or near them? Near friends? In the city? Suburbs? Countryside? An over-55 community? A Life Plan Community? An apartment? A condo? A mobile home? In the North? Down South? Out West? How will I manage if a catastrophe should happen to me or mine? A heart attack? Stroke? Debilitating illness? Bad fall? Car accident? Alzheimer's? Bankruptcy? Stock market collapse?

What about my finances in the future? What are my assets? What about health insurance? Do I have enough money to meet my needs? How do Medicare and Medicaid work for me? What about long-term care insurance? Dental care? Prescriptions?

Then we may go deep: What is important to me? House? Possessions? Memories? Friends? Talents? Activities? Experiences? Travel? Grandchildren? As I get older and lose energy, whom or what will I want to focus on? If my health is compromised, what will give me a sense of satisfaction every day?

Age, health, family, and future. Thinking about these questions is important. Envisioning, exploring, reflecting, and choosing – these tasks take time. But the more time we spend thinking, evaluating, visiting, and learning, the more confidence we will feel in our decisions and the happier we will be.

Right now, you may be healthy, have assets to fund reasonable choices, and have time to explore future options. You have choice and control. The best time to think about the rest of your life is now.

Serendipity Happens: Lester

Lester never envisioned moving to a retirement community. With a carefree personality, tall lanky frame, silver hair, blue eyes, and a tan, weathered face reflecting a lifetime of activity, he had let life's events carry him along. He shared his story one evening at dinner:

About a year ago, my wife got sick and then died within a week. She was only ninety-one. My son said, "Dad, where will you live now?" I was already having trouble remembering things, and that house was looking kind of big ... and lonely, too.

A few days later, I was trimming some bushes at the back of my house. Nearby was a door into the basement, and in the

6

basement was a beautiful shop I had made. It was full of vises, drills, saws, built-in tool racks, everything. I was proud of that shop! My back yard was visible from the road. A man driving past pulled over and called out, "Are you selling your house?"

"Yes, I guess I am," I said. I'd put the For-Sale sign on the front lawn just that morning. "Do you want to take a look?"

"How much do you want for it?"

I forget the price now, but he seemed to like whatever I said.

"Do you want to look inside?" I said.

"Sure."

Since we were right by the back entrance, I led him into the shop. He took a good long look – up, down, all around. His shoulders relaxed.

"I'll take it," he said.

"But you haven't seen the rest of the house – the upstairs, the kitchen, the bedrooms."

"That's okay," he smiled. "With a fabulous shop like this one, I can make the house into anything I want!"

The next day, I visited the daughter of a friend of mine from way back. He had died, and she kinda looked out for my wife and me. When she heard I'd sold my house, she said, "Let's take a ride and find you a place to live."

Driving past Rolling Meadow, she said, "Let's check it out." We had picked up her friend, another woman I knew, so there we were, two middle-aged women and over-ninety me, asking whether they had a room for me.

1: Dignity, Choice, Independence

"As a matter of fact, we do," said the person at the desk, and the next thing we knew, we were looking at what they call a studio apartment. I figured I was just along for the ride, so I stayed in the background. "What do you think," asked the employee, and my friend said, "I think it's great. We'll take it."

"Wait!" I piped up. "Don't I get to say a word about this?"

"Well," my friend said, "you need a place to live, and this looks nice. I think you'll like it here. What do you think?"

Turns out she was right. I've been here around two years now. I can't believe it, but I'll be ninety-three this year.

Many times, I've asked myself this simple question: Am I happy? The answer is always the same: Yes, I am.

Wait! Did he say ninety-three? Lester's lithe gait and cheerful demeanor showed me how well the community lifestyle suits him. I'm glad that Lester had a little help from his friends.

Think of older people you know: Where do they live? How are they managing? What resources are available to them, and do they, can they, use these resources? How well prepared are they for future health problems? What are their concerns?

For anyone in their older years, the future is now.

You did everything you could to nourish your children, careers, and passions. In your thirties, forties, fifties, your hard work provided success even amid the difficulties that may have come. Having cared for others, you have earned a lifestyle now that focuses on your own needs, interests, and talents. No matter your age and stage, you need to know that good things await you.

1: Dignity, Choice, Independence

What is *home*? More than walls and a roof, *home* is where we feel safe, comfortable, and happy. We can feel at home in a room, a suite, or a mansion. Stripped to essentials, disregarding size and décor, *home* is a place of dignity, choice, and independence. Years ago, you were helping your children find the college or career path that suited their talents and interests; now you can pursue your retirement home according to your own abilities and personality.

Email to friends: Two days ago, on Don's birthday as it happens, Don and I accepted an apartment at Rolling Meadow Life Plan Community. The apartment and the entire facility are about perfect for us, and we are optimistic about moving there. Our future home has two bedrooms, two full bathrooms, a moderate-sized kitchen, a sunroom, and a balcony. It's on the top floor overlooking a sweeping vista of tree-covered hills. We may move in three months, perhaps less. And then we'll sell our house. The timing is a little sooner than expected, but this apartment is too tempting to pass up.

A good day starts with a
positive attitude and a great cup
of coffee in your favorite mug.
Sometimes that positive attitude
takes two or three cups.

2: I Don't Want to Move

The universe is like a safe to which there is a combination, but the combination is locked up in the safe. — Peter De Vries

Questions: What are some ways I can assess my life? I don't really want to move, and so why should I even consider it? I can take care of myself in my own home, or can I? I tended to my children and helped my friends: why can't they do the same for me? If I'm willing to consider moving, what are my housing options? Why shouldn't I just downsize to a smaller home or move to an Over-55 community?

"I'm too young to think about getting old."

We're never too young to think about the future.

Some things are inevitable:

- If we live long enough, we will get old.
- Like it or not, things change.
- Our bodies and/or our minds will decline.
- Money is important.
- Planning pays off.
- I can take charge of living my best life possible.

2: I Don't Want to Move

You and I are formidable in experience and in numbers. Look at who we are:[4]

Some of us are **The Silent Generation**. Born between 1925 -1945, we are generally more cautious than our Jazz Age parents. From us have come rock music, iconic filmmakers, TV legends, beat poets. Our predecessors, dubbed the **Greatest Generation** (born 1901-1924), went through the Great Depression and World War II and produced JFK, LBJ, Nixon, Ford, Reagan, Carter, and G.H.W. Bush. President Joe Biden emerged from the Silent Generation. Although my husband may at times disagree with the *silent* part, I belong to the Silent Generation.

Others are **Baby Boomers**. Born 1946-1964, we filled the Post-World War II bubble in which 72.5 million boomers were born in the U.S., plus 6.3 million more immigrated to this country. Presidents Bill Clinton, G.W. Bush, Barack Obama, and Donald Trump are boomers. Baby boomers are the huge group of new retirees who grew up with higher levels of education, greater optimism, more financial success, and more comfortable lifestyles than their parents had. My sister is a boomer.

Generation X, born 1965-1980, include our own middle-aged children and, so-far, no President. Due to debt, only 36 percent of Generation Xers have more wealth than their parents. In 2028, Generation Xers will outnumber Baby Boomers. They will inherit both the problems and the plusses of retirees' benefits: notably, senior-housing growth and expanded health care services. They pay attention to news stories about Social Security and retirement age.

---

[4] "American Generation Fast Facts," *CNN Library*. CNN.com, updated August 17, 2019. Accessed June 2, 2020.

As for the younger generations, **Millennials** were born in 1981-1996. By 2014 their numbers had grown to 83.1 million, exceeding the 74.4 million Baby boomers. They are the most diverse as well, with nearly half (44.2 percent) representing a racial or ethnic group. My high school students were millennials. **Generation Z**, also called **Gen Z**, were born around and after 1997; Gen Z are our grandchildren and great-grandchildren, to whom we leave our personal, political, cultural, environmental legacies.

Sixty-five is not the beginning of old age but the beginning of "mature middle age." A cardiologist says she divides her older patients into the "young-old" and the "old-old" with no numbers attached, explaining that one patient may be "old at sixty-eight" and the next "young at eighty-eight." Even the definition of *old* is hard to state. How old do you feel? I have always felt younger than my chronological age, and maybe I look it too, yet I know people younger than I am who look and act older. "Age is just a number," they say. My bicycle-riding 86-year-old friend Harry says, "forty is the old age of youth; eighty is the youth of old age."

Most older people are less interested in how *long* they live than in how *well* they live. Ironically, however, living well promotes longevity. Think about it: fewer responsibilities, less stress, nutritious diet, health support, and more time for friends, family, and physical activity – these things help you relax and enjoy life. Wouldn't you like to be described as movie director Steven Frears was, as a "canny old vet with a youthful verve"?

We enjoy every experience we can. Chuck, a motorcycle owner since he was sixteen, now at eighty-four has bought an electric-assisted bicycle for pedaling around his Michigan terrain. "My legs don't like the hills anymore," he laughs. After a bout of brain cancer that was an unwelcome surprise, Ed enjoyed a solo, six-month postretirement camping/canoe trip exploring the American West and northern Mexico. Sylvia Marie at seventy-seven is so involved with her pottery business that she has no time between art fests and museum talks even to consider moving her studio and herself. "I feel young, I'm healthy, I love my home, and I'm too busy to think about next week, let alone the future," she enthuses.

However, each of us at some age begins to transition from "I can take care of myself" to "I may need help" to "I can't manage very well anymore." Our children or friends spot a memory lapse, or we ourselves notice a decline in energy. Perhaps our handwriting gets shaky, we start dropping things, forget to pay a bill, or have fender-benders every few months. Maybe the newspapers go unread, we eat popcorn for dinner, or pull the shades and stay inside most of the time. Perhaps we stumble and nearly fall. Maybe we are tired of cooking all the meals or cutting the grass, especially on hot, humid days. At some point, we take stock and realize, yep, I may be starting to get old.

"I want to stay in my house."

Like most people, you may not want to move. In your present home, you have years of memories, comfort, neighbors, along with access to stores, bank, bakery, gas station, library, park, pizza. You're amid all your things. Financially, you can manage – maybe you've even paid off the mortgage – and you can handle repairs and upkeep. Pressed about future changes in the neighborhood or in your energy or health, you confess, "I just don't want to move. It's such a hassle. How would I get rid of all my stuff? Where would I go? It'll probably cost too much. I'm happy where I am." Less open about deeper feelings regarding wellness and safety, you may say, "I'll be okay. I'm healthy. Nothing will happen to me. I don't want to think about it."

Then something nudges you to admit things have changed. A wife returns at 4:00 PM from bridge with friends to find her husband taking his pulse, looking distressed, saying, "I don't feel well. My heart's been fluttering all day." A woman realizes that, after she has shopped for, brought home, and carried in the groceries, she does not feel like putting them away, she'll wait 'til later. Sometimes a medical emergency becomes a family alarm:

> **Returning from checking the sound system in the auditorium adjacent to the health wing, Don told this story: Do you remember Rhonda[5] from the pharmacy in town? I ran into her coming out of Skilled Nursing. I thought she looked stressed and asked if I could help. She said she was visiting her father. He's in his eighties, and he fell in his home. He wasn't found for two days. The ambulance crew said he'd broken his hip and was badly dehydrated too. In the hospital they replaced the hip and repaired a broken bone.**
>
> **He lives about ten miles away, and he's here to recuperate. Rhonda doesn't know whether he'll want to return home or even whether he'll be able to. She doesn't know if going back home is what he wants. She is worried — she doesn't know whether they'll have to sell his house and his things. She's dealing with a lot of uncertainty.**

You too may have stories of friends or family who have had slow declines or sudden emergencies. Perhaps it was a health issue that mushroomed into catastrophe. A neighbor in her eighties had a painful sore on the bottom of her foot that turned out to be melanoma. She had X-rays, MRIs, blood-draws, excision, plastic surgery. These procedures lasted for months, not counting mental stress for her and her family, especially her husband who had to take over the

---

[5] "Rhonda." All names are fictitious. All stories are real.

household chores and drive her to all her medical appointments. What does a person do?

Can a senior stay healthy at home? Yes, health care in the home is usually available, both short-term and long-term. Is your house suitable for a person in compromised health? Perhaps a rearrangement will suffice, like setting up a downstairs bedroom, clearing away extraneous furniture, removing loose carpets, and putting kitchen, laundry, bathroom items close to hand. The house may require renovations like widening doorways for wheelchairs or walkers, attaching grab-rails in bathrooms and along hallways, adding enhanced lighting, modifying bathroom fixtures, installing a chairlift on the staircase, or providing inside-outside electronic security features.

If the resident should require live-in help or companionship, someone may have to hire a contractor to enlarge the house to accommodate the person, and someone may have to set up a system to find, supervise, and pay that companion or team of helpers. Will liability insurance be needed? Are there tax consequences?

So far, these concerns have been for the person's physical health and safety. What about the social issues that underlie good mental health? When people can or should no longer drive, how will they enjoy the benefits of spending time with others? Who will provide transportation, and at what cost in money and inconvenience? Withdrawing from the company of others, some seniors begin dwelling on their problems or their boring routine or even start retreating indoors, sometimes turning their cheerful home into a bleak cave. Those who live alone risk the problem of loneliness or, worse, isolation.

Isolation is not so much *being* alone as *feeling* alone. We all have had times when we felt disconnected from others or uncomfortable in a group, but an unremitting feeling of isolation can lead to depression. There are other causes of depression, too. For example, chronic health conditions such as diabetes, cancer, Parkinson's disease, and heart disease can produce a gloomy outlook, as can fatigue, physical or emotional stress, hearing loss, and certain medications. "The Centers for Disease Control and Prevention (CDC) estimates that nearly seven million Americans over the age of sixty-five experience depression each year. ... Depression is not a normal sign of aging. It is a medical condition that needs to be diagnosed and treated promptly."[6]

Hiring Help in Your Own Home

As well as feeling isolated and lonely, you may find that staying in your home can be a financial burden. In fact, *new* expenses may mount up. You may need help with the house – cleaning, laundry, shopping, meal preparation, lawn and gardening maintenance, snow removal. You may need help with personal care – dressing, showering, using the bathroom, cooking, eating. Hiring helpers requires scheduling, coordination, supervision, interacting with a variety of providers, as well as legal concerns of liability and personal security.

Some people use the services of an in-home senior care agency. Agencies with comprehensive in-home care may be able to provide such help as part-time housekeeping, cooking, laundry, transportation, barber/beauty salon, giving medications, and full-time live-in

---

[6] Leisure Care. https://www.leisurecare.com/resources/continuing-care-communities-vs-life-plan-communities/, accessed May 25, 2020.

care. To cover all your needs, you may need to hire more than one agency.

However, trained workers arriving at your house may not be the same people each time, and indeed their agencies discourage their workers from developing personal relationships with clients. Also, you pay the agency, and it pays the workers: for example, you may pay thirty dollars an hour, from which your well-liked helper may receive eleven. Thus, your helper is earning only a fraction of what you think you are paying her or him. In fact, she or he may be underpaid and – to earn a living wage – possibly overworked. Ideally, you will like your helpers, and they will like you. Their care for you and their training will hopefully be above average and their personalities pleasant. Unfortunately, satisfaction is not guaranteed.

The decision to hire help in the home warrants much investigation and thought. Advantages of hiring in-home care include a fee-for-service feature that allows you to pay only for what you need and the sociability of having various people coming and going. Disadvantages include uncertainty about who will arrive to do what and the need to keep track of the schedule and bills.

Helping Mom Decide to Move

My family experienced a huge hurdle when our Mom, a sturdy, independent widow of pioneer Norwegian stock, preferred to continue living at home. After experiencing precarious health and unable to live alone for at least the next six months, my brother, sister, and I conferred across the country by phone. Then my sister Sarabeth and I traveled to Mom's riverside cottage to figure out what to do.

With Mom resolute about staying home among her things, Sarabeth used pen and clipboard to chart their dialog. After two hours of empathetic questions and attentive listening, Sarabeth summarized: "It sounds like this is what you're saying: You want to be home. You realize it is unsafe to be here alone. You are willing to have help. You can afford to hire someone. You realize that someone should be here all the time, day and night. You have a bedroom for that person, and you are willing to share the bathroom." Mom was pleased that all her thoughts and wishes had been heard.

Together, they listed expectations that Mom would have for a helper: companionship, light housekeeping, meal preparation and cleanup, and driving Mom where she may need to go. Finally, they charted expenses based on Sarabeth's guesstimate of the hourly cost of service. Twenty-four hours a day, seven days a week yielded an unexpectedly large sum. Gulp. All three of us were surprised at how high it was.

Then Sarabeth said that one person alone could not be expected to carry the responsibility 24/7, so that a rotation of at least two, and possibly three, workers would be necessary. Bigger gulp. We had all envisioned just one caretaker, not two or three.

After the discussion concluded for the day, we phoned our brother Sid to update him. Having studied her finances, he affirmed that her modest income and savings were sufficient to pay for any care she would need.

The next morning, Mom startled us. "I've been thinking about it, and I just cannot have strangers living in the house with me. It gives me the creeps. I couldn't relax. I couldn't take a nap. I'd be fretting constantly that she's going through my things. I know this idea just won't work."

Meanwhile, late on the day before, Sarabeth and I visited an assisted living facility where we learned that an attractive room was available. To our surprise, and to Mom's as well, she could live there for a lower cost than what she would pay for twenty-four-hour care at home. She would have her own room with a key, three meals a day, and plenty of independence to spend her time as she wished.

Not needing our input, her sensible mind led her to make the decision: "I cannot live alone. I do not want outsiders living with me. I can afford to live in assisted living and still keep my house for when you visit. Yes," she said, "I can see that I'm better off moving there." She did not like this decision, but she saw the sense in it.

Mom thrived in her studio apartment. She socialized at meals and at activities while, in her cozy nest, she happily enjoyed her own television, two sewing machines, and the computer whose word-processing capability thrilled her.

Mom's move to assisted living compared to watering a wilted plant and watching it stretch upright and bloom again. After precarious health, she gained three years of satisfying life. She enjoyed having less stress, new friends, stimulating activities, and abundant personal privacy. After a short illness, Mom died peacefully just a few days before her eighty-fourth birthday. Never having expected to live even to be eighty, she had enjoyed her final years as a gift.

"My children will help me."

For most of the elderly living in their own homes, the responsibility of caregiving goes to one or more family members. "A 2020 study by The National Alliance for Caregiving (NAC) and AARP found increasing numbers of adults who are serving as unpaid caregivers for a senior. From 2015 to 2020, that number grew from 43.5 million to 53 million. This unpaid care accounts for about sixty-five percent of the care provided to seniors today, with the balance being provided by paid caregivers."[7] Almost one-fourth of these unpaid caregivers are helping more than just one person in the household.

Ironically, it is the caregiver who often pays a personal price. The caregiver may have to shorten her/his work hours or even give up a job, costing not just lost wages but lost contributions to retirement and savings funds, possible debt, and possible loss of health insurance. The caregiver may have to curtail her/his own social life, time with spouse and children, and other personal interests including exercise and fitness. A caregiver may be putting her/his own physical health in jeopardy: illnesses such as cancer, hypertension, diabetes, and clinical depression sometimes correlate with physical or emotional stress. In truth, a woman who gave four and a half years of dedicated service to a beloved father-in-law before he died said she had no regrets but described the experience as physically, mentally, and financially exhausting.

You probably want housing where you can live your final years in comfort, health, and safety. Keep in mind, however, that as you age, your children do, too. When you are in your eighties, your children may be in their sixties, possibly dealing with their own health issues. "When I can't take care of myself, who will take care of me?" said my vigorous eighty-seven-year-old neighbor while telling me about her sixty-two-year-old son whose loss of peripheral feeling had mystified his doctors. "I always figured he'd be helping me, but now I can't count on that to happen." Another woman had moved to

---

[7] Breeding, Brad. "How Senior Living is Evolving to Meet Future Demand," https://www.mylifesite.net/blog/post/how-senior-living-is-evolving-to-meet-future-demand/ June 1, 2020, accessed June 20, 2020.

Pennsylvania to stay near her daughter whose career had recently brought her there. A year later, soon after the mother had made new friends and activities, the daughter was transferred to Connecticut. Both households moved, again. The daughter's needs complicated her mother's desire to be near her.

However, let us assume an adult daughter or son can help. Before committing to give unpaid care to a parent, relative, or friend who can no longer live safely alone, the person would be wise to consult with others. For example, a professional financial advisor can analyze how the caregiver's potential loss of income plus extra expenses may affect her/his own financial security both now and into the future. An attorney can point out legal ramifications when one person is moving into the home of the other. For example, will the house or grounds need to be renovated and, if so, who will pay for the changes?

If there are other family members involved, they should discuss key issues: Who will do what, for whom? Who will pay for what? Who else can help, both paid and unpaid, and how often? What will happen if the older person – or indeed the caregiver – should fall ill or need surgery, incur a disability, or suffer memory problems that would interfere with the success of the retirement plan? Is everyone aware that nearly a third of at-home caregiving lasts five years or more? How long will this commitment be?

If you are the older person, think about your future: remaining at home in your oldest years may pose tough decisions. Beyond the possibility of unwisely using your money, you may have difficulty keeping abreast of legal affairs, financial paperwork, federal, state, and local taxes, changes in medical services, revisions in Medicare and Medicaid regulations, not to mention computer and television frustrations. Whom will you trust to care for your increasingly complex needs? Equally serious, when your caregiver is your spouse, who is also likely to be elderly, the ongoing stress of your home health care can be so detrimental to your spouse's own health that he or she may face a health crisis, too.

Yes, providing care at home may seem your most comfortable and least costly option for senior housing. After all, you already have a system to pay for home maintenance and maybe your mortgage is paid off. You want to stay in your familiar and comfortable house. However, other considerations demand attention: your emotional cost of accepting in-home assistance from your child, relative, or friend; the financial and personal stresses on an unpaid caregiver; and, as years go by, your eventual, inevitable decline in physical and/or mental health.

On behalf of both you and your in-home caregiver, take a realistic look at all aspects of life care in your home. You have physical, emotional, social, financial, and legal reasons to proceed only with great caution.

Hopefully, you and your family will find a win-win solution where everyone feels that the best care decision has been reached. There is no right answer for everyone. Paramount is the need to assure your own safety, comfort, and security not just this month or this year but for the rest of your life.

And yet, aging at home can be done. Here are the words of a woman who assured her own comfort, safety, and happiness on her own terms, in her own home. Sophia had taught fifth grade for thirty years, caring deeply for each child and keeping in touch with many of them over decades. Petite and perfectly dressed, every hair in place and a sparkling smile for everyone, she has for all her life carefully considered every decision. For example, she accompanied me along my journey to learn about retirement communities, even joining me to interview a home health-care agency when I was considering staying at home. Sophia details her experience in this reflective essay:

Deciding to Stay in My Home: Sophia

As a child, I lived on a large farm in a very rural area of Erie County PA. Our closest neighbors had no electricity or plumbing. Until eighth grade I attended a one-room school that had a hand-pump, a wood stove, and two outhouses. I spent my days roaming the woods and fields learning to identify birds, butterflies, and flowers. I became a lover of nature. Helping my father feed the animals and tend the farm garden, I learned the responsibilities of caring for one's own property.

Later when my husband and I moved to Bucks County PA, we agreed that we wanted a country setting for our home. A wooded lot in a semi-rural township was our perfect spot. With our architect, we chose our home's features, and we finished building it in 1969. Fifty years later, I am still comfortable and happy in this same home where, harking back to childhood, I created a natural setting for the birds, monarch butterflies, and flower gardens whose care is an important part of every day for me.

My mother's example inspired my own independence. In her seventies, retired and widowed, she decided to leave western PA and come to live near her grandchildren. My husband Lyman, Mom, and I made a joint purchase of land from a neighboring farmer, and Mom built a lovely ranch home while, at the back of her property, Lyman built the horse-barn he had always wanted. Mom's arrival turned out to be a wonderful move for my kids, having their grandma next door.

As she entered her nineties, Mom let us know that she was determined to stay in her home and would not consider a retirement community. Like me, she enjoyed her flowers and birds and was comfortable in her home. With a little help from my sister Judy and me, she did in fact live at home until she died at ninety-nine years of age.

In my life, two major transitions have occurred. First, Lyman passed away in 2008; he was only seventy-three. At the same time, some of my friends were moving to retirement homes. They shared two reasons with me: their overwhelming worry about home maintenance, which their husbands had always handled, and the equally overwhelming loneliness they were experiencing.

For me, these concerns were not a consideration. I was not lonely. I was busy babysitting my two grandchildren and, a couple of times each year, flying to visit my two other children and their families. I was enjoying my gardens and spending evenings with Mom. As to home maintenance, over the years Lyman and I had assembled a list of local people whom I could call upon for any problem, including driving me to and from the airport as needed.

My getting older required more serious thought. Mom passed away in 2012, and my grandchildren had grown old enough not to need my frequent help. By then, more friends were moving. I decided to tour several retirement communities.

Although they seemed welcoming, I knew I preferred my own home. Even so, I had to consider what would happen if, like my mom, I needed daily help. My daughter lives hundreds of miles away, so the mother-daughter situation was not the same. One friend had told me that she moved because she did not want to burden her sons with caring for her. As close as I am to my sons and their wives, I realized that the possibility of imposing on their lives was a valid concern. I also remembered how, after Mom gave up driving, I took her to all her doctor appointments and social events. Who would drive me? Transportation became another question. And there was one more worry – in her last few years, Mom had become unable to handle stairs, and I have a two-story home.

I found solutions to all these concerns:

A close friend told me about Friends Life Care, a Quaker-sponsored plan for home assistance. After attending informational meetings and having my lawyer carefully check the contract, I signed up. When needed, a care-coordinator arranges in-home care. So far, I used this feature when a caregiver stayed overnight after my knee surgery. The plan supplies a Life Alert® device which I wear in case I need emergency assistance. Ironically, my coordinator's name is Hope Joymaker! Isn't that a great name for that position?

Both my parents were mentally sharp their entire lives, and I admit to feeling confident that I have inherited that trait. Turning my attention to physical fitness, I set myself a daily workout: before I even rise from bed, I do a series of leg/arm extensions and flexes. Later, I walk the treadmill and work the weights that Lyman had set up for us in the basement. My son Gregory's family in western PA and I all wear smart-devices to measure our activity, and each week we compete to reach 10,000 steps a day. It is a fun and friendly multi-generational contest. At my age of 83, I am the oldest competitor.

My son Rupert, living just a few miles away, exchanges a smiley-face email with me every day at 9:00 AM, our way to say, "I'm fine; how are you?" An advantage of computer-connectedness is that, on their computers, all my children can check my whereabouts every day to know I'm up and active.

When I may have to give up my car, I will use a car service – I already have the Uber app on my phone. If I cannot manage stairs, I can move into Mom's ranch house. Looking ahead to my possible need of one-floor living, I kept her home and rent it out. As part of the rental agreement, I take responsibility for lawn and garden maintenance there. Usually, this task is left to the tenant, but looking forward, I want to be sure that, should I live there, the upkeep fits my standards. In a great twist, my newest tenant grew up on a farm and has a gardening family, so she helps me with this work that we both enjoy.

Keeping in touch with my three children, their spouses, and my seven grandchildren by text and FaceTime® adds the personal contacts that one needs when living alone. My sister Judy and I talk every day to share little happenings in our lives. Being fortunate to have close relationships with my family, I never experience feelings of isolation or loneliness.

I am comfortable with the choices I have made, knowing, however, that I must be open to new options should my health change in the future.

Lately, a friend asked how my children felt about my decision to remain in my home. To my surprise, I had no idea! I had kept them apprised of my decision-making but had never solicited their advice. I texted each to ask their opinions. All three replied immediately, and their responses were very affirming. Suzanne wrote that if I am happy and safe here, it was a good choice. She recalled how her Gram had enjoyed staying in her own home with my help. Gregory said he is happy that I was independent

enough to decide on my own, and he feels it is the right decision for me. He added that his kids, Leo and Cassandra, are glad that I am here at home. Rupert just said, "I am all for it!" These positive responses make me feel good!

Sophia has accounted for her physical, mental, and emotional needs for now and the future. I expect she will listen to her inner voice of caution and to her wise children to assure that she lives in comfort and safety. She has found her own secure way to achieve a win-win.

At the end of this book is a list of "Helpful Sources on the Internet." It presents information about LPCs, Over-55 and Senior Co-Op Housing, Remaining In Your Own Home, Caregiving at Home, Long-Term Care Insurance, Financial Information for Seniors, Help for Veterans, Help from Your State, Help from Medicare/Medicaid, and a Life Expectancy Calculator.

3: Options for a Life Plan

Question: *Where can you live so that you will be both happy and healthy? What are "Life Plan Communities"? How do they work? Who runs them? How does the application process work? How can I look at Life Plan Communities without making any commitments? How much money are we talking about?*

You consider the pros and cons of staying in your home, which may be your desire, versus the alternative, moving to a smaller place. Maybe your family or your friends are urging you to plan ahead. They point out that now is the time to provide yourself with a home with all the essentials you will want and need: a comfortable lifestyle, safe surroundings, and – most important – complete health support for the rest of your life no matter what may happen.

Use this "essentials" checklist for each housing option:

_____ **Will I be comfortable?** friends, activities, services, furniture, layout, outdoor access?

_____ **Will I be safe?** design, neighborhood, trustworthy helpers?

_____ **Will I be healthy?** accidents, illness, daily assistance, nursing care, memory care?

Many housing options are available.

You can downsize to a **smaller home**, getting a head start on the daunting task of sorting through your possessions.

You can **buy or rent a house or apartment** (1) in a traditional setting or (2) in an Over-55 senior living community where you can enjoy meeting people with similar interests and live amid features such as a clubhouse, swimming pool, walking paths, tennis, badminton, bocce, or a golf course. Financially, you may find that the sale of your family home more than covers the purchase or rental of a smaller place. Over-55 homes may already have wide doorways, assistive devices like handrails and grab-bars, one-floor living, and perhaps familiar features like sunrooms, patios, attached garages, and attractive landscaping maintained by someone else.

If your house has low equity and your savings are limited, you can explore moving into **government-subsidized housing**. Low-income housing may have simpler floor plans and fewer communal services, but residents live in an inexpensive setting that provides respectable housing at a modest cost. The supply of affordable housing is limited but is growing as providers become aware of the great need. Waitlists are long!

If you have compromised health, perhaps needing a walker, wheelchair, medication monitor, overnight oxygen, or personal care into the future, you can investigate moving to an **assisted living** facility. There, you have privacy and independence amid a safety-net of helpers. You may choose a studio (one room with bath) or a small apartment (one bedroom with living area, kitchen, and bath). Provision of meals, housekeeping, and laundry services lighten your responsibilities. Personal services like hair care, banking, transportation, social activities, and wellness programs provide convenience and stimulate you physically and mentally.

Thus, you can downsize to any of these smaller homes that provide interesting, engaging, helpful features. They will all address two of the three essentials for senior living: comfort and safety. Living there, you gain more time to pursue your interests because you have fewer responsibilities. For example, when the roof leaks or the dishwasher floods, management repairs the problem. Maintenance people care for the property inside and out. Living among compatible people, you have physical comfort, less stress, and, yes, more fun.

A good place to begin thinking about housing is with cost comparisons. You will benefit by completing a chart like the following:

> Note: This chart and the other charts in the book are available in PDF format at the book's web site.
>
> https://LovingLifeInALifePlanCommunity.com/

3: Options for a Life Plan

What are my costs at my current home
vs. senior-housing alternatives?

Cost/Feature Each Month	My Current Family Home	Condo, Town-house, Over-55 (purchase)	House, Apart-ment (rental)
Mortgage payment/rent			
Homeowners' Association dues			
Utilities: Electric			
Gas			
Oil			
Water			
Sewer			
Trash/recycling collection			
Homeowners Insurance or Property Insurance			
Flood insurance			
Property Tax			
School Tax			
Security system			
Cable TV			
Internet service			
Phone service			
Housecleaning			
Lawn & garden service			
Snow removal service			
Maintenance (average)			
Repair/Replacement (average)			
Social: Gym/Club membership			
Magazine/Newspaper			
Pool Maintenance/Fees			
TOTAL			

Completing this chart is a way to compare costs while also as-sessing what you spend now and what you require. For instance, thinking of the costs of heat and property tax may inspire you to ask whether you need to continue supporting extra bedrooms, a family room, and a large property. Why pay for what you no longer use? If you give up your lawn and gardens, what could you enjoy instead? Local parks? Travel? Tennis? Volunteer work? Embroidery?

As you set forth to discover where to live, you may expand your personal definition of *home*.

"Home. The word seems inseparable from houses now, and from notions of domesticity and ownership. Yet when I looked it up, I learned that its original meaning referred not to a building or even a geographical location but to a state of being – a place at the heart of the real. A place from which worlds could be founded; a place where meanings are made. ... my sense of 'home' had changed. I no longer thought of walls and windows but a feeling I could build and share. ... home appeared less tangible, more movable, less fixed – and oddly, more immediate." – Helen Jukes[8]

As Helen Jukes suggests, in our busy working lives, *home* is a place, but in our childhood and retirement, *home* is a feeling. In "The Death of the Hired Man," poet Robert Frost said, "Home is the place where, when you have to go there, They have to take you in." He described feelings of obligation and respect. When a friend moved alone into her modest little farmhouse apartment, she created a cozy spot that said, "Welcome, relax, be yourself." Looking back to

---

[8] Jukes, Helen. "Behind the Book: Making a Home Among the Bees," *Book-Page*. May 2020, 14, 15.

those few years on her own, she reflected that she was defining not just her furnishings but her attitude to life.

Locating a good college or workplace for your child is important; for you, finding outstanding retirement living is vital.

What are Life Plan Communities (LPCs)?

Looking ahead, consider the housing option that gives you not just comfort and safety but also **health care**. Like your treasured antique car or your grandmother's vintage sewing machine, your body may also need special care as time goes by.

When your housing contract includes "life care," you benefit.

Think about it. You want to be as comfortable, safe, and healthy as possible for the longest time possible: into your seventies, eighties, nineties. You will not want to move again. You will want to meet new people and learn new routines. In a life plan community, you can settle down where you have the friends and healthcare you need, forever. Such places not only exist, but they are also proliferating. Why? Because you are part of a tsunami of retirees. Over twenty-eight million Boomers retired in 2020, and, ever since 2011, that number has been increasing annually by about two million.[9]

Baby boomer retirements have spurred the growth of Life Plan Communities. What sets LPCs apart is their offer of a "continuum of care." If you qualify for admission, then, for the rest of your life no matter what happens to your health, you are guaranteed the care and services you need.

More senior citizens than ever before are moving to LPCs. Many of these residents have educational and achievement levels higher

---

[9] Fry, Richard. "The pace of Boomer retirements has accelerated in the past year," November 9, 2020. Pew Research.

than in previous times. Active minded, they want more than just a place to live. They want services and amenities that used to be considered luxuries, and they want on-site medical care available in case they should need it. They look for comfort and attention equal to or better than they are already accustomed to having.

When seniors consider Life Plan Communities, they enter a competitive LPC market in which they hold the aces and kings. Thus, salespersons in LPCs promote housing deals, special services, and dining selections to entice residents to move to their communities. Along the way, most residents find that their new homes are better than they had expected and sometimes superior in unexpected ways.

Considering Life Plan Communities

A friend, Elaine, wrote: "Why did the phrase *life care* appeal to me? In 1991 – while teaching and with children in college – I had cancer, chemo, and radiation. That harrowing year heightened my appreciation of living fully and as long as possible. Over the years, the fear of disease had lessened, and my zest for life had strengthened. Having moved five times during my marriage, I figured that this move to a retirement community would be the last one ever – 'except for the cemetery,' as my husband quipped. I focused on Life Plan (Continuing Care) communities where we could live comfortably in times of good health, or recuperation from illness or surgery, or in times of frail health fraught with physical or mental impairment. I figured that, living in such a community, we would never have to move again, and we would be as safe, comfortable, and healthy as possible."

Elaine continued: "In 2008, my eighty-one-year-old friend Sally joined me on a quest to explore six communities. For each, we called the Marketing Department to ask to be invited to an upcoming Open

House, and they were happy to include us. An 'event' usually includes a delicious brunch or lunch, sometimes with current residents seated at each table to answer questions and just mingle with us 'prospectives.' Then a marketing manager or an administrator describes the community and its financial requirements, and she/he answers all questions. Finally, the sales representatives divide the prospectives into small groups and give tours of residences and features like craft/hobby rooms, entertainment centers, library, pool, and gym. Sally and I enjoyed these outings."

Within months, Elaine had collected folders filled with colorful pamphlets, number-filled charts, floor plans, checklists, plus notes of what she liked and disliked at each community. Each talk added insights into how these communities work financially, presented tips about downsizing and moving, and gave assurances about how a "life care" facility benefits its residents. Each tour let her imagine how her husband's and her personalities and lifestyle might work in this community. Each tasty meal promoted the dining services and friendly atmosphere in that community. In fact, during that year, a recent graduate of the local culinary arts school said that many newly trained chefs work at retirement centers. "Believe me," she said, "Grandma and Grandpa are eating very well at these places!"

After each of her visits, her husband questioned her, absorbing details yet adding few thoughts of his own. He did not want to commit to anything, but he wanted to know everything she had learned.

As Elaine had once done with her children on their college tours, she used her notes to create comparison charts of important elements: her categories were not just costs and location but size, ambiance, amenities, services, meal plans, and "red flags." Meanwhile, when she told her daughters about this quest, they were excited. Jane said, "That's great, Mom! It'll be just like going back to college, but no exams!" Her husband teased: "Jane means she's glad she won't have to take care of you." "Why should she," said Elaine. "I figure the best gift we can give our children is that we will take care of ourselves. They have their own busy lives to lead, and – if we do our part – we'll have busy lives too."

Not everyone looks ahead to a distant future. Many people move to a Life Plan Community on very short notice. At dinner soon after his arrival, Joseph, a tall, lumbering man with a deep voice and gentle, unassuming manner, shared how he dealt with every newcomer's plight of learning lots of new names, and then he told how he happened to move to Rolling Meadow.

Not a Cocktail: Joseph

I've been here two months, so there are still a lot of names to learn, but I have a way to remember. Years ago, I realized I was good at sales, so I took a Dale Carnegie course to improve my skills. Standing in front of the class, the instructor told us to imagine him wearing underwear that he named "bright red longjohns." Then, stretching his arm toward us, he said to envision a tall, icy Tom Collins cocktail in his hand. His name? "John Collins"! I use that trick all the time now.

Before I came here, my wife and I looked at a community with cottages. We liked the idea of having not just a garage but also a patio so I could barbeque steaks. Then she got sick, and that plan ended. She died six months ago, but before she died, she told me to move. "You'll need help" is the way she put it. So, I followed her directions, and I like it here well enough – and I hope there's a barbeque that I can use now and then....

Whether the reasons are immediate or long-range, people find their ways to a retirement community by coming for a visit ... and sometimes by listening to their wives.

An Introduction to Life Plan Communities (LPCs)

LPCs are for seniors (1) who have accumulated financial strength by means of home ownership, savings, and investments, and (2) who understand that their needs may change over time such that they may require assisted living or skilled nursing. In a Life Plan Community, you are assured lifetime healthcare without relying on children, relatives, or friends; couples know that, should one of them need care, the other can continue to live just a few minutes' walk away.

The newer name *Life Plan Community* seemed to attract baby boomers who were looking forward not to a "rest home" but to a place filled with active, robust life. Whether it is called a *Life Plan Community* or a *Continuing Care Retirement Community*, such a place provides comfort, safety, and health for the rest of your life.

Each Life Plan Community (LPC) offers all three stages of retirement living:

(1) In **Independent Living**, you reside in an apartment, townhouse, or cottage with all the freedom and independence you always had but without the stresses of home maintenance.

(2) If or when your health should falter, you can transition to **Assisted Living** (Personal Care[10]). For example, you may be falling, forgetting your medications, or no longer able to bathe on your own. You may need help just in limited ways. You can still drive your car and enjoy all your activities and friends in the community.

(3) If your health declines or you need short term rehab care, you can move to **Skilled Nursing**. Many Communities also offer **Memory Care** for residents with dementia including

---

[10] In Pennsylvania, *Assisted Living* and *Personal Care* are two distinct levels of care. They have different licenses and are defined differently by regulation. Other states are more likely to have just one level: Assisted Living.

Alzheimer's disease. In Skilled Nursing and Memory Care, you receive round-the-clock nursing and attendant care tailored to what you need.

In a Life Plan Community, receiving a "continuum of care" means that you, or both of you, can move just one time to a place that provides comfort, safety, and health support for the rest of your life.

Thus, a Life Plan Community promotes itself as an adult leisure community with social and recreational amenities. It integrates private living units, hospitality services, and health care. Some communities feature an elegant lifestyle of leisurely pursuits while others feature their homey, relaxed, informal lifestyle. Some cost more, some cost less. The more you learn, the happier you will be.

A Little History

In the 1990s, the need for Life Plan Communities was clear:

> Someone did a study at Duke University a few years ago because Duke was building a retirement community. "Why are you choosing a continuing care community? What are your reasons?" And the study showed that the number-one reason is peace of mind. Knowing that if something should happen, I can get care, primarily because I don't want my children to worry about me. And, let's face it, unless this nation returns to getting families back together, closer together, and I don't see that happening, senior parents will always have to rely on someone else to take care of them. So having that peace of mind was the number one reason. The second reason was maintenance-free living. Wanting to be able to shut the door and travel and know that everything's being taken care of. Where else can you get that but in

a continuing care community? Health care and food service were also high on the list.[11]

"Having peace of mind" means a lot to a person:

No Slip-ups: Irving

Irving had lived at Rolling Meadow for over twenty years. One wintry afternoon, seeing him people-watching in a sunny corner of a lounge, I asked if I could join him. His bright eyes, quick smile, and relaxed bearing made conversation easy. Noting the recent snowfall outside, he enjoyed sharing a tale that he called "No Slip-up for Me":

Snowstorms are usually forecast well ahead, and like everyone else I look forward to staying indoors and watching the snow-globe outside. Just last week, my neighbor Jonathan said, "There's nothing like watching the snow falling outside while I'm sitting in the hot tub at the Wellness Center."

But going outside into the ice and freezing rain is another matter.

Not too long ago, I went to church one Sunday morning, and, when I was ready to leave, I saw that rain had frozen everywhere. I held back because I knew I was wobbly on the ice. I was nearly ninety, and I definitely did not want to fall. A fellow parishioner offered to take my keys and drive my car from the parking lot back to the church door. Talk about a godsend!

But when I parked here at Rolling Meadow, I still had to cross the ice to the building. Had they salted the macadam yet? I didn't

---

[11] Harrigan, John E., Raiser, Jennifer M., & Raiser, Phillip H. *Senior Residences: Designing Retirement Communities for the Future.* John Wiley & Sons, Inc., NY., 1998.72-73.

know. I decided to sit in my car for a while and think about what to do.

Fortunately, Mrs. Kitchener happened to be at her window. She figured out my dilemma, and she called Security. Within minutes, a maintenance worker in his electric go-cart arrived at my car and walked me safely back to the door. My good neighbor Mrs. Kitchener – and Security – had saved the day.

> You are not a drop in the Ocean.
> You are the entire Ocean, in a drop.
>
> – Rumi

I haven't lost all my marbles yet,
but there is definitely a small
hole in the bag somewhere.

4: Talking About Money

Questions: What's the difference between a for-profit and a not-for-profit LPC? ...between Life Care and Fee-for-Service contracts? How do I know when I'm ready to move to an LPC?

For-Profit or Not-For-Profit?

As a business, a Life Plan Community is either for-profit or not-for-profit. One is not better than the other, but it's helpful to understand the difference:

A **for-profit** organization pays taxes based on its net income. It can raise money from private investors and, in exchange, give equity or dividends to shareholders, who expect a return on their investment. It is a money-making enterprise led by a business hierarchy.

A **not-for-profit** organization is exempt from paying income tax. It is dependent on the income received from residents and can seek donations from individuals, foundations, and businesses. Strict regulations oversee the ways funds are distributed and operations are managed. **Not-for-profit** LPCs are founded by churches, local business leaders, and universities. They are operated by a developer or by a manager serving as the Chief Executive Officer (CEO).

For years, **not-for-profit** Life Plan Communities, formed as a service to their residents, kept a low profile. Often, the admissions person was like a tour guide who showed clients around without necessarily giving reasons why *this* was the place to choose. However, with a multitude of boomers retiring, the market was expanding. New LPCs were being built and advertised. Becoming competitive, new **for-profit** LPCs created sales and marketing departments to "sell the product," offering Open House events, brochures, and specials to attract new residents.

Not-for-profit and for-profit LPCs have things in common. **Not-for-profit** LPCs, conveying an aura of excellence because they originated as church or community service ventures, joined their **for-profit** brethren in this way: they both operate on sound business principles. Like their competition, new **not-for-profit** LPCs must manage well in a competitive market on behalf of their mission to care for their residents. Both **for-profit** and **not-for-profit** Life Plan Communities strive to balance high ethical standards of excellence with responsible corporate financial goals.

Note: Don't confuse LPCs with for-profit Assisted Living facilities that have no option to progress to skilled nursing. When you exceed what they can offer, you must move out to a facility that can offer that care level. Many of them will not accept Medicaid patients and will require you to move if you become unable to afford their monthly fees.

Understanding the financial foundation of your prospective Life Plan Community is important.

Life Care or Fee-for-Service?

It is also important to understand the two basic types of contracts. They are called **life care (Type A)** or **fee-for-service (Type C)**. Each Life Plan Community (LPC) has one financial structure, sometimes more than one.[12] Once you understand the two basic contracts, you can deal with the variations you may meet. Please note that in most communities, you also pay an **entry fee**. It is not part of your contract. The entry fee can be relatively modest or rather expensive, for it is based upon the zero to ninety percent refund that will be returned to your estate after you die or if you move.

In a **Life Care contract** (also called **Type A**), you pay a large entry fee and a substantial monthly fee; and, for that same monthly fee, you will receive whatever care you may need for the rest of your life. For example, your "life care" contract covers all health services, including the box of tissues at your bedside when you may be on life-support. Except for cost-of-living adjustments made annually to your monthly fee, what you contract to pay at entry will remain the same year after year regardless of level of care. You are contracting for life care. In fact, with the approval of your financial advisor, you can relinquish the long-term care insurance policy you may have been paying for because you will no longer need it.[13]

In the other type of financial plan, a **Fee-for-Service contract** (also called **Type C**), you also pay an entry fee and an inflation-adjusted monthly fee. However, your monthly fee is based on your level of care, from least to most expensive. Independent/Residential units have the lowest fees because you take care of your own health needs. Assisted Living has significantly higher fees because you are receiving assistance with activities of daily living that you cannot manage on your own. For example, aides may be assisting you with your pills, dressing, laundry, eating, or other daily needs. Skilled

---

[12] Type B is Modified Life Care and Type D is Rental, but they are not commonly available.

[13] For this and all other recommendations about money, you should seek the counsel of a professional financial advisor.

<u>Nursing</u> has the highest fees because you receive a great deal of personal and medical attention.

In a Life Plan Community, the three levels of care are these:

(1) Independent Living – **least expensive.**
(2) Assisted Living – **more expensive.**
(3) Skilled Nursing, which may include Memory Care for residents with dementia – **most expensive.**

What about your **long-term care insurance** policy? You may have bought it years ago, and your annual premiums may have become considerable. Will you need it? At a fee-for-service community, yes, you will want to maintain your policy because you may need it. All Life Plan Communities offer services including nursing care, health-aide assistance, physical and occupational therapies, laundry, housekeeping, and more. At a **Fee-for-Service** community, where all services are billed individually (including that bedside box of tissues), having a **long-term care insurance policy** can be essential. You may not need it in Residential (Independent) Living, where you care for yourself, nor in Skilled Nursing, where Medicare/Medicaid may supplement your costs;[14] but your long-term care insurance very much benefits you if your doctor says you need to move into Assisted Living. In Assisted Living, you are responsible for covering the additional costs. <u>You must hold onto your long-term care insurance until you are sure whether it will benefit you at the Life Plan Community you are choosing</u>. Caution: Before relinquishing your policy, ask the advice of a professional financial advisor. Be aware that your LPC may require that you maintain your Long-Term Care policy.

---

[14] Medicare is not guaranteed, covers skilled nursing only, and has a coverage time limit of 100 days. Medicaid requires you to qualify financially.

Variables: A few Life Plan Communities require **no entry fee** and only a monthly rental payment. Others present a choice of payment plans; for example, the same community may offer Life Care at one price and Fee-for-Service at another price. For all LPCs, their contracts, fees, coverage, and services vary widely.

You must ask questions during your research and visits because understanding the type of contract each LPC offers is essential for your planning. A worthwhile goal is this: you should be able to explain the contract terms to a friend or your family. Additionally, ask advice from your attorney and/or your financial advisor. Be sure you understand the deal before you sign papers or give money.

"I'm not ready yet."

Question: Why can't I just wait to move to an assisted living facility until my health deteriorates, which may never happen?

Answer: Because you will have waited too long. You may have to move suddenly, without choices, without the chance to make friends and enjoy your new setting. Moving now to a Life Plan Community, where you have a continuum of care, allows you to build relationships in Independent Living. You will have complete independence until or unless you need assistance. When you or your spouse may need to move into Assisted Living or Skilled Nursing, you will make the transition smoothly within the same familiar community of friends, services, and amenities.

Talking about fee structures and contract types can be daunting. Maybe you think you will never become old anyway, so why bother. But the fact is that you are likely to live longer, and better, in a Life Plan Community.

All Life Plan Communities are different. Like choosing a college, a neighborhood, or friends, the more you see, the more you know.

Nearly One Hundred: Cosmo

I wonder whether, thirty years ago, Cosmo expected to become a centenarian. Of medium height and build, balding and bespectacled, he blends into a group – until, that is, he lights up in conversation:

In a gathering place facing a wall of windows overlooking the main entrance, ensconced in a red wingback chair, Cosmo was reading the newspaper. He looked up alertly as a passerby queried, "How are you today?"

"I'm feeling pretty good," he said. "And that's how I like it, 'cause I want to hang around for another year and a half. That's my goal. Because then I'll be a hundred. That's right! I'm ninety-eight now, and on July 12 this year I'll be ninety-nine, and one year after that I'll be one hundred."

Walking by, Theresa interjected, "Do you feel ninety-eight, Cosmo?"

"No," he said, "not in my brain. My body does, though. That's why I use this walker – my balance isn't good. I wear hearing aids. In a crowd I can't hear, but when I'm talking with just one person, I hear pretty good."

Just then, the mail truck arrived at the curb. The carrier rolled in a cart full of new mail, then departed with the day's outgoing box. Theresa asked, "Cosmo, didn't you used to work in the post office?"

"No," he said, "that was my son Cyrus. Cocking his head toward the pony-tailed young woman at the mail-truck, he said, "You know, he was the one who trained this carrier. Cyrus taught her for three years before she came over here. I guess she's been

4: Talking About Money

bringing us our mail for nearly eight years now. When Cyrus graduated from high school, he worked in a shirt factory for a while. One day a buddy said they were hiring at the post office, so Cy applied and passed the test. He's retired now.

"What about me? I worked at a plant in Philadelphia every day for forty-three years. I commuted into the city and back again – more than an hour each way. Oh, the stories I could tell about that! And now I've been retired for thirty-three years."

The math added up: high school, two years in the service, then work, and finally a long retirement. Cosmo has had a satisfying life and wants more. Way to go, Cosmo!

As a prospective resident, you are shopping in an open market. Each Life Plan Community wants you, and you want what's best for you. At each LPC you like, you are welcome to ask, "What does this place cost? Can I afford it?"

To live in your Life Plan Community, you will pay up front to cover your costs for the rest of your life. How long will you live there? You can expect to live longer than you may expect, for a couple of reasons: fellow boomers are setting records of robust health, and you are moving into a less stressful lifestyle. For example, you may reside in your LPC for as many years as your children's K-through-college educations – twenty years or more. Financially, you are investing in your future.

The LPC you are evaluating is checking you out too. How? As potential residents, you must qualify for the community in two ways: your health and your finances.

Mental and physical health assessments are done by the applicant's personal physician and by the clinic nurse and/or social worker of the community. For instance, to observe your gait and balance, the nurse may follow you as you walk to the meeting room. To check your mental awareness, the social worker may ask you to describe where you are in this building and to count by sevens, backward, from a hundred: do not worry – you can take your time, and three or four subtractions will suffice. (I had done a lot of mental math when I was teaching, so when I rattled numbers down to "sixty-five," he grinned and said "Stop – You've lost *me*!")

These evaluations are done to assure that the services of the community are a good fit with what you need. For example, a spouse might need Memory Care, but its location is not on the campus, making it inconvenient to visit. In this case, perhaps it would be better to choose another community.

Further, the application requires a detailed description of finances including all income, bank accounts, investments, property values, long-term care insurance if you own it, debt, and a listing of all monthly expenses.

Ideally, you have accrued money for years so that you can live the retirement lifestyle that pleases you. If you have a stock/bond portfolio, you have shepherded it carefully toward your retirement goals. What about the vagaries of Wall Street? T. Rowe Price said the following:

> Approaching Retirement and the Unknown: For investors nearing or in retirement, it can be unsettling to experience a volatile market. History has shown that bear markets have typically been followed by healthy market recoveries. While investors are in the thick of market downturns, it may be difficult to stay the course and believe things will turn around. Try to resist the urge to make drastic changes in portfolio strategy when

markets become more volatile, especially early in your retirement horizon.

By following a conservative withdrawal approach early in retirement and planning for systematic adjustments along the way (if needed), retirees can weather the markets and have a truly fulfilling and enjoyable next phase in life.[15]

> **I have seen a medicine**
> **That's able to breathe life into a stone,**
> **Quicken a rock, and make you dance canary**
> **With spiritedly fire and motion.**
>
> **– William Shakespeare**
> ***All's Well That Ends Well*, II,i**

---

[15] "Heading Into Retirement During a Down Market: A conservative withdrawal approach is part of a sustainable retirement spending plan." *T. Rowe Price Investor*. Summer 2020. 6-9.

I like to make lists. I also like to
leave them on the kitchen counter,
then guess what's on the list
while at the store. Fun game.

5: More About Money

Questions: *How much do I have? How long will I live? What's my cost up front? How much each month? How can I have enough money for whatever may happen? What about Long-Term Care Insurance? Who can help me decide? What if I want or need to move?*

Evaluating Assets and Longevity

Listing all your assets is like taking a deep breath: you are preparing for something big. Entering a Life Plan Community requires a large investment akin to purchasing a house for cash – you pay a lot up front. The time has come to spend some of your savings to secure your lifestyle in a place that will provide comfort, security, and health-support for as many as twenty to thirty years ahead.

It can be a shock to have to present to strangers the details of your finances. It was to me, anyway. Completing the paperwork took Don and me hours, over several days. When we were done, though, we had a current assessment that we could use for any other community that we might also apply to. This task, carefully completed, helped us see our financial situation clearly.

Sample: Financial Statement for Application to a Life Plan Community

Applicant:	Joint	#1	#2
MONTHLY INCOME			
Social Security	X		
Pension	X		
IRA/401(k) Distribution	X		
Annuity Payments			
Other income			
MONTHLY EXPENSES			
Insurance premiums			

Auto			
Health			
Life			
Long-term care			
Medicare Part B/C/D			
Prescriptions			
Mortgage/Rent			
Other expenses			
LONG-TERM CARE INSURANCE DETAILS			
Benefit period			
Elimination period (number of days before payment begins)			
Daily benefit for Assisted Living			
Daily benefit for Skilled Nursing			
Is there a benefit inflation adjustment rider?			
Premium			
Assumed inflation rate on premiums			
ASSETS			
Primary residence: current market value			
Mortgage balance			
Home equity lines of credit			
Total equity (market value minus loans)			
Name under which residence is deeded			
Other real estate			
Savings account balance			
Checking account balance			
Money market account balance			
Certificate of deposit value			
Interest rate			
Stock values			
Mutual funds			
Bonds/bond funds			
IRA/401(k) value			

Distribution amount/frequency			
Annuity value			
Life insurance (cash surrender value)			
Burial reserve			
Other assets			
LIABILITIES			
Credit Card Debt			
Student Loans			
Car Loans			
Personal Loans			
Medical Debt			
Other Debts			

Whew!

After the community receives your application, its Financial Officer reviews the numbers to advise the Admissions Committee about your ability to pay for whatever levels of care you may need for your estimated lifetime. The older you are, the shorter your presumed life expectancy, and thus the less funding may be required.

How long will you live? You can guesstimate by asking how old your parents were when they died and how healthy you are. You cannot foresee accidents and catastrophes. You can check your longevity on a Life Expectancy calculator online: for example, Social Security has one at https://www.ssa.gov/OACT/population/longevity.html. To my surprise, I learned that I may live until I am 89.4 years old, exceeding my previous guesstimate and meaning I would outlive my parents by five years. My mother had never expected to be eighty, yet she lived to be eighty-four. I expect never to be ninety, but – who knows!

Alas, because salespersons do not disclose actual numbers, you are unlikely to get an answer to the question, "How much money will I need?" Instead, you will hear, "Why don't you apply, and we'll let you know." However, some financial advisors suggest guidelines like these:

At one time, a person needed a monthly *income* of about two and a half to three times the monthly fee, with other assets a secondary consideration. If the monthly income were insufficient, then other assets were included in the evaluation. Another formula estimates that your total assets should be twice the entry fee, and your monthly income should be one and a half times the monthly mainte-nance fee. Overall, the financial department looks for an income/as-set mix that assures your ability to fund your needs in every level of care: Independent Living, Assisted Living, and Skilled Nursing.

Keep in mind that, due to inflation, the monthly fee may increase annually, usually three to five percent, sometimes more.

New residents usually move into Independent Living and, in the future, may transition to Assisted Living and/or Skilled Nursing. Only about twenty percent of residents are likely to use nursing facilities for longer than a year. The average age at entry to a Life Plan Com-munity is mid-seventies to early eighties. I recommend moving in your mid-sixties to early-seventies so that you can use your good health and robust energy to move and to make friends and pursue activities; indeed, you may lengthen your years of active enjoyment of life. If you wait until you *need* to move, you waited too long.

Assessing your needs will be cumbersome yet gratifying, like be-ing deluged with cold water on a hot, sunny day. Now, you are ready to take the next step. The sooner you explore Life Plan Communities and move to one, the sooner you can enjoy the benefits of your less stressful lifestyle and discover how well you feel as you look confi-dently to the future.

Music: Claire

Let's take a break from money to enjoy a story. Claire is one of many long-time residents whose life brims with activity:

Upright in her bearing, when Claire walks, she glides and sways at the same time. You can't live at Rolling Meadow without hearing Claire play hymns on Sunday mornings and play familiar tunes at lively sing-alongs before residents' meetings. In a recent November, I emailed Claire to ask whether she had sheet-music for Rudolph the Red-Nosed Reindeer. "Let me look," she replied, and after fifteen minutes she called to say "Yes." I explained that I was writing humorous lyrics for a large bridge group to sing. "Oh," she offered, "I'd be glad to come and play the accompaniment." What a generous surprise! Two weeks later, I visited Claire with the new lyrics. Immediately, she noticed I'd revised some of the notes and rhythm.

"Can you read music?" she asked me. I said, "Yes, but I can't play the piano." "Well," she said, "I'm entirely self-taught." At my curious expression, she told me her story:

Did you know that I was an orphan? My three brothers and I grew up in an orphanage. I was six when we went there. The orphanage had a big room for activities and meetings, and in the corner was a piano. I spotted it right away, and that's all I wanted to do. I never was interested in dolls or games or toys, just that piano. I remembered how my mother could play anything she wanted to, and how I'd sit next to her and bang on the upper keys. In the orphanage, I spent as much time as I could at that piano, experimenting and listening and amusing myself.

When I was about ten, a music teacher came to the orphanage. Someone there must have told her about me, and, thinking

I might have talent, she offered to give me lessons. Well, after three or four weeks, she gave up on me. "That girl won't learn anything! All she wants to do is play notes her way. She's stubborn and way too independent." That was the end of my music lessons, forever.

In junior high school, the music teacher explained how written music works. The lines, the staff, sharps and flats, rhythm. I loved learning that! I'd been wondering how one person could write down what she hears so that someone else could understand it. Now the melodies I was playing by ear could have permanence on a piece of paper. Because I could already play, I learned to read music by playing what I already knew.

I love to play. My husband was a lot older than I was. When he and I were looking at retirement communities, the reason I liked Rolling Meadow was that I knew they needed me because I love to play the piano. We moved into our apartment nearly twenty-five years ago — I was only sixty then. My apartment is still beautiful. I have a huge collection of music because when people downsize, they give their sheet music and music books to me.

I've noticed that when people do what they love, the whole community benefits. Years ago, we had a man, Samuel, who lived to be a hundred and two. On his one-hundredth birthday, we had a big party for him, with a hundred lit candles on his cake, and for a joke we had a local fireman rush in to pretend to blow out those little blazes. Sam had marveled that he'd lived so long. But then he figured it out: he said he prays every day for everyone here. Praying was his passion, and playing piano is mine. So, yes, I feel that, when we have an opportunity to do what we love, we thrive.

...And More About Money

Each community has its own fee structure available for the asking; often you can find it on the community's website. You can use the following chart for your notes about each LPC that captures your interest:

Fees at Life Plan Community

	First Occupant	Second Occupant
One-time Entry fee		
Independent Living Monthly fee		
Assisted Living Monthly fee		
Skilled Nursing Daily fee (or) Monthly fee		
Cost of Living adjustment applied to monthly fee (percent)		

When you move into Independent Living, you are buying – among many other features – peace of mind. You will have the health care you need, if indeed you should ever need it. This comfort is important to remember when you think about the cost of your Life Plan Community: your investment provides value beyond what is measured in just dollars.

How to Decide?

With many options for how to live the rest of your years, you can prioritize key factors. Important questions include these:

- o How much money do you have, including the cash total you will receive from selling your house?
- o How long do you expect to live?

o   What kind of health insurance do you have, and how fully does it cover catastrophic illness/injury?
o   Do you have long-term care insurance, and how much coverage does it offer, for how long?
o   How healthy or possibly needy do you expect to be until your death?

This last factor – your health – is tricky, for it requires you to imagine the element of risk. What do you think are the odds that you will need help because you no longer drive or must use a walker or wheelchair? How likely is it that you will need care due to an accident, debilitating illness, recuperation, or dementia? If you are married, partnered, or if you are caretaking a disabled child or grandchild, you must evaluate the odds that your beloved spouse, partner, or child may also need expensive end-of-life care. You want to die peacefully in your retirement home, but may you face expensive end-of-life issues that you cannot predict and do not want to think about? Among your acquaintances, do you know someone who was struck unexpectedly by a life-changing accident or illness? Can you imagine something like that happening to you?

If you are in good health when you are exploring Life Plan Communities, you realize that, in choosing either a Life-Plan or Fee-For-Service contract, you are making a financial gamble: shall you pay a large monthly rate starting now but never increasing, or shall you pay now a lower rate that could mushroom to a lot, later, if your health should decline? When you roll the dice of future health, what do you see? As for the once-only entry fee, which I discuss in the next section, shall you contract to pay a higher versus a lower fee? As an insurance or financial advisor may say, or as Clint Eastwood said in *Dirty Harry*, "You've got to ask yourself one question: 'Do I feel lucky?'"

Please note that, if you or your spouse, partner, or adult child already has health issues, then your salesperson, financial advisor, or lawyer can give you essential advice regarding these decisions. Their expertise can guide you through the pros and cons for each financial and legal aspect of your pathway of choices. Each salesperson can counsel you as to the fee structure at that facility. All your hard work will pay off: when a Life Plan Community accepts your application, you know that the Admissions Committee has deemed your finances to be enough for your lifetime. In return, the community promises never to turn you out because of inability to pay. You will have a *Life Plan for Continuing Care.* Good for you!

Serendipity: Naomi

In the Dining Room, a reminiscence enlightened our lunch. With a rounded face and generous girth, Naomi filled her electric wheelchair not just bodily but also with smiles and wit. That day, when our conversation meandered to the strange paths that life can take, she recalled this happy tale from decades past:

When my son was in college, he babysat the children of one of his professors. For two summers and part of one year, the professor and his family lived in Switzerland, and they asked my son to go with them, which he did. My husband and I visited them there several times and liked the country very much. I practiced my German and learned some more.

Later, at Disney World, a young woman kept eyeing me from across the room. Finally, she approached me and said, "Excuse me, but you look exactly like my mother." Her mother lived in Switzerland! Her little girl accompanied her, about three years old. I asked whether the child could speak English. "No, not a bit," her mother said. I said, "Does she speak German?" "Well," the mother said, "she'd understand some of it."

So, in German I said to the girl, "That's a very pretty dress you're wearing," and she smiled. The dress was decorated with images of Mickey Mouse and Minnie Mouse. "Do you know the Mickey Mouse song?" I asked. When she shook her head, I said "I'll sing it to you in German." She loved the song, and I sang it again to teach it to her, and then we sang it together.

The mother asked if I could write the words and tune for her to take back to Switzerland, and I did. We've kept in touch all these years. That little girl is now a doctor in Switzerland.

More about Entry Fees

Have you recently attended or heard tales about going to settlement to transfer property? The flurry of papers among realtor, buyer, and seller boggles the mind. With so much to take in, all at once, it's no wonder that the final handshake is such a relief. Because moving to a retirement community is a legal transaction, having a framework of what's coming can help. You can expect a frenzy of documents, all based upon decisions you have carefully made.

You chose your basic contract type: Life Plan (Type A) or Fee-for-Service (Type C). In travel terms, you signed up for a "package tour" versus a "pay as you go" itinerary. In dinner jargon, you order a *prix fixe* or an *à la carte* dinner.

Another Word about Long-Term Care Insurance

If you choose Fee-for-Service, a huge plus is to have the long-term care insurance that you have been funding for years. It supplements the cost of Assisted Living, which – if you need it – is expensive and does not qualify for Medicare. At a Fee-for-Service community, having long-term care insurance can be a dealmaker. One retirement community rejected friends of mine until the wife added, "Oh, did we mention that we have long-term care insurance?" Their application was then accepted.

Because Don and I had long-term care insurance policies, and because we have a financially modest lifestyle, and because our roll of the dice came up with "healthy for the duration," we chose a fee-for-service path. Thus, we pay for what we need, and if deteriorating health should befall us, we are prepared to use our income, long-term care insurance, savings, and investments to cover the higher costs of care that unforeseen circumstances may require.

So Much to Think About!

In your financial planning, you consider the size of the Entry Fee. Which entry fee and which refund amount, if any, will you contract for? Your entry fee can vary from nothing to quite a lot. The amount you choose will correlate with the amount of your refund, ranging from a refund of zero to a refund of ninety percent. Thus, it is important to keep the numbers hat on your head a little longer.

When the contract ends at your death or, occasionally, at your decision to move elsewhere, you will have contracted for you or your estate to receive a refund. Some Communities offer a sliding scale of refund percentages: a larger cash entry yields a larger refund; a lesser amount yields a smaller refund, or none. For example, if you enter with a fee of $376,000 with a 90% refund, yielding to your estate $338,400 – you would have given a large sum for a large return, relinquishing only $37,600 to the community; or you could pay considerably less upon entry, let's say $195,000, with no refund expected, relinquishing all $195,000 to the community.

Each community has charts showing the terms they offer. Sometimes, Marketing has found that having many columns filled with numbers causes confusion rather than enlightenment. For example, the chart at Rolling Meadow showed only three Entry Fee Refund options: 0%, 50%, and 70%. If you prefer a refund percentage that is not shown on the chart, your salesperson can find out whether that number works for their Financial Officer. Just ask. Don and I did, and we received the percentage we wanted.

Residents have various financial goals: Some people need to keep their fees as low as possible. Some prefer to keep control of their money to invest hoping for greater returns. Some want to assure their money is secure for their estate. After you study this chart to see how the sums interrelate, you may develop a sense of which approach may work well for you.

Examples of various refund percentages for a person with $376,000 available for an Entry Fee plus a Possible Investment[16]

Funds available to you to invest elsewhere	Lump sum at entry	Amount retained by the community	Refund upon death or moving elsewhere
$0	$376,000	$37,600	@ 90% = $338,400
$146,000	$230,000	$172,500	@ 25% = $57,500
$181,000	$195,000	$195,000	@ no refund = $0

The sale of your house provides a major resource to help fund your entry fee. To help future residents use the cash value of their homes to fund their entry, some communities offer a grace period of up to a year to complete the house sale; other communities make different adjustments. You can ask about this adjustment.

---

[16] If you knew when you were going to die, and what return on investments you could earn, then you or your financial advisor could figure out your better choice. For example, at an eight percent return, Don calculated that he and I would have to live here nine years to break even; at a four percent return, sixteen years.

As for the refund, the contract describes how and when it will be dispersed. For example, there may be the stipulation that, should the resident deplete all funds from other sources, then the value of the refund will be used to pay for care. For a couple, the value of the refund can be used to support the needs of the primary resident or those of the surviving partner. After one or both residents have died and the apartment has been occupied by a new occupant, then the untapped portion of the refund will be returned to the estate.

It is important to ask all your questions so that you understand and can explain what your entry fee and possible refund will be. With confidence in your decision, you can then proceed.

A Misunderstanding: Sherman

Along their paths of life decisions, most people try to do the right thing all the time. As an earnest young man, Sherman did his best, and then fate took over:

I asked, "Sherm, did you participate in vigorous sports like football when you were in high school?" His deep voice rumbled, "No, not much, because the war was getting started then." At ninety-plus years of age, Sherm meant World War Two.

At seventeen, right after graduation, he had joined the U.S. Navy and served in the Pacific, where he had harrowing experiences that he didn't much like to talk about. But his mind was not at a battle this day, and he went on, "At the end of my enlistment, I nearly signed up for a career, but it didn't work out. I was a radar-man, and they said I could take a test and if I did well, I could stay on after the war ended.

"So, I took the test, and they said they'd let me know in two weeks. Well, two weeks went by, and I wrote to ask about it because my discharge date was coming soon. I didn't hear a thing from them, so I went ahead and processed out of the Navy and went back home to Pennsylvania. A few weeks later, I got the letter that I'd passed the test and could report for duty. But it was too late. I didn't see much point in going back."

Memories were in his mind now. "My brother had been in the service too. He was a radioman. I was radar, he was radio. I joined the active reserves, and he was in the regular reserves. After I was working back home as a civilian, the Navy wanted to call me back because they needed more radarmen, but the notice I received to report put my name with my brother's serial number, so I ignored it. I ignored the second letter too. Then the third letter said they'd arrest me if I didn't show up, so my brother and I both went down.

"We pointed out my name and his serial number. What to do? Well, the Navy solved the problem. They called my brother to duty, not because they wanted a radioman, but because they'd listed his serial number! It all worked out okay, though. He served on a seaplane-tender off the coast of South Korea and found he liked it. After he got out, he worked in a radio station in Baltimore and ended up working at a television broadcast station in upper New York State."

More Financial Details

You may want to know about the following:

(1) If you should move or die within the first few years in your Life Plan Community, most contracts will give a full refund of the entrance fee, less a percentage per month. Ask your salesperson.

(2) If you are contracting for pre-paid health care (because you have chosen the Type A contract for life care), then the portion of your fees that covers health care may be a deductible medical

66

expense that you may claim when you itemize your income tax. Ask your financial advisor.

(3) Correspondingly, if you contract for life care, you likely will not need the benefits of any long-term care insurance and can save money by cancelling the policy. Ask your financial advisor.

While the Admissions Committee scrutinizes your finances, you can return the favor by studying the finances of that Life Plan Community. You need to request a copy of their Disclosure Statement, which is an informational booklet that explains in non-technical language who and what are involved in the organization and management of the community. Also, you can request a copy of their audited financial statement. Then you can review these documents with a qualified financial advisor.

You should ensure that the LPC can cover its expenses out of its operating income.

Additionally, ask for their occupancy rate: a ninety-percent occupancy signifies good health.

Also ask whether there is a Benevolent Care Fund in place to help support residents who, through no fault of their own, have run out of money.

Finally, ask the cost of the monthly fee, which is a set amount based upon the size of your living unit, how many people are living in it, and sometimes its features or location. For example, I know of one community that adjusts its fee for an apartment depending upon the popularity of the floor, proximity to central services like the Dining Room, and the view. At every community, the monthly fee is adjusted periodically according to fluctuations in the economy, so ask about changes:

1. How often are adjustments made? (once a year is typical)
2. What were the increases for each of the past four years? (three to five percent is reasonable)
3. Do increases align with the rate of inflation?

I recommend that you frequently visit your future LPC. Every time you speak with your salesperson, you learn more. For example, you may discover that "move-in specials" are being offered: some communities give free meals for three, six, or twelve months; others pay for the entire move from house to apartment; others pay for a team to pack your household and then unpack everything in your new home; others offer a lump sum, multi-thousand-dollar move-in discount. In one way or another, the Community Wants YOU.

Be sure to save all the written material you receive, including advertisements and brochures, for you are entitled to have any service or amenity offered in writing at the time you sign the contract.

Discuss with your salesperson any special needs that you may have so that costs for reasonable accommodation will be included in your contract. For example, if you know now that a bathroom door must open *out* to the hall rather than the usual *in* to the room itself, then that simple adjustment can be made before you move rather than your being charged five hundred dollars for it after you have moved.

As you think all these thoughts about money, keep in mind your top priority: you are investing in lifetime care. Keeping **life care** in the forefront is like polishing your crystal ball to have a clear view of your living well whatever may happen in your future.

Final Thoughts...

Many couples who are blessed with longevity decide together how and where to spend their last years. After decades of shared experiences, sometimes a person finds that she or he is unexpectedly alone: a spouse, partner, friend, relative may die, move out, or become disabled. Living alone may not be a first choice for most people. Although it is possible to live like a hermit in any dwelling, in a friendly retirement community there is joy – and personal safety too – in neighborly sharing and caring.

Thinking ahead about one's older years requires these things:

- time (two to three years, or more)
- imagination (envisioning yourself in a variety of situations)
- information (research, personal visits, interviews)
- discussion (with family, friends, professionals)
- thought (evaluating, estimating, questioning)

It is a big help to acknowledge that the only constant in life is *change*. Like it or not, our bodies, our minds, our living circumstances are going to change. Further, statistics prove that ten out of ten people will eventually die. We can ignore or deny these facts – lots of people do – or we can embrace end-of-life issues and make plans to live our best possible lives.

> **Go forth on your path, as it exists only through your walking.**
>
> **– Augustine of Hippo**

Can someone point me in the
direction of the greenhouse?

6: It's a Business

Questions: *How will I benefit from seeing a Life Plan Community as a business? What should I know about its financial goals? About marketing and sales? About dining services? How can I assess the senior communities I visit and keep all the information clear in my mind? Why should I evaluate what I want versus what I need? What are the pros and cons of the many aspects of each senior community, things like housing options in Independent Living, services within the senior community, and outdoor amenities?*

"What Do I Want?" Madeline

Everyone is different in every way. The more one knows about himself/herself, the happier he or she can be, and especially in retirement when so many choices are available. Here's one woman's reflection:

> I had thought that the educational level of the residents was an important factor in my decision as to which community to choose. I had wanted to be amid college-educated professionals so that I would find friends who would converse at my intellectual level. That criterion was high on my list.
>
> Then I noticed that retirement communities filled with college graduates were expensive. Touring them, I felt the inner me rebelling against patterned wallpaper in the hallways, elegant light figures in the public areas, and abundant stemware on white-

covered dining tables. Examining what I really wanted, I realized that a formal, fancy lifestyle was not it.

Where I felt comfortable were the communities that were low-key, plain, with as much diversity as possible. When all is done, my happiness depends not upon college degrees, job titles, former addresses, or outward appearances. Feeling at ease with others, hearing interesting stories and poignant life experiences, these qualities are what make life meaningful.

How did Don and I choose Rolling Meadow from the many fine retirement communities in our area? We started by creating a gallery of impressions from all the open houses, talks, and tours we attended. From my abundant notes about independent living, I made extensive comparison charts, even including notations about my emotional reaction to each place ("too formal, notably welcoming, felt like long corridors inside a ship, loved the grounds").

At Open House events, we picked up cues about how the staff and residents behaved among each other and toward us "prospectives." For example, on apartment tours when our group passed residents in the hallways, the salesperson often greeted them by name and made short inquiries like "How's your grandson doing this semester?" Since each table at the brunch or lunch frequently included a current resident, we could ask why they liked this community, what activities they enjoyed, what suggestions they could offer to newcomers. When we were shown facilities like the swimming pool, billiard room, art center, exercise room, auditorium, chapel, health suite, library, workshop, and craft room, we imagined which of these places we ourselves would enjoy using. Viewing apartment owners' hallway displays, we gathered impressions about the interests and personalities in that mini neighborhood.

Displaying Who You Are: Glenn

A couple of years ago, my parents moved into Brooksby Village, one of the largest retirement communities near Boston. ... The management at Brooksby installed a shelf in the hallway next to each apartment door. The shelves are small, about two feet long and one foot deep, and are all the same. But the residents use them in endlessly varied ways.

My parents chose to display a blue glass vase (a gift from me) and, somewhat incongruously, a little bronze Komodo dragon. Some shelves feature sentimental cards or teddy bears or flowers, real and artificial, or mementos of loved ones. ...

As a result, when you walk around Brooksby Village, you always know where you are thanks to those landmarks. But it's obvious that the shelves and their contents are serving a purpose higher than mere navigation. Despite the diversity, they have a single message. They say to passers-by: This is us.

... Wherever we are, at whatever age, we have an impulse to tell people who we really are through a few resonant objects.[17]

A Life Plan Community Is a Business

As an enterprise, the purpose of a Life Plan Community is to find and keep its "customers": that is, to provide its residents with a worry-free, enjoyable lifestyle in independent living with access to excellent health care should the need arise. A successful LPC sustains itself by means of happy residents and contented employees.

---

[17] Adamson, Dr. Glenn. "A Retirement Home's Lessons in How to Keep in Touch: A curator finds much to admire in the creative exuberance of the objects in these halls," *The New York Times*. September 22, 2018.

For the LPC, risks begin with the property itself. The Chief Executive Officer and his or her team make management decisions to stay current with countless and changing regulations, maintenance, renovations, new construction, landscaping, and so on.

Another risk involves marketing: the community must keep selling new units and reselling vacated ones. After all, vacancies reduce cash flow, and reduced income affects management. The competition for prospective residents is huge. The offer of attractive comforts, abundant services, and friendly, experienced staff results in high occupancy, which benefits everyone. Hotel-type attentiveness, high quality dining, and up-to-date amenities differentiate LPCs from nursing homes.

Outstanding health care is critical, for every resident should feel that, if he or she must ever go into care, the experience will be pleasant and professional. In fact, the primary attraction of an LPC is its enhanced lifestyle that guarantees personal and/or nursing care for the life of the resident. The goal of an LPC, therefore, is to offer a range of service and style at a level of excellence to suit an array of expectations.

In an LPC, the staff and employees are an integral part of the "family." Working full-time or part-time in the business office, dining services, health care, building services, transportation, and housekeeping, they regularly update their training and enjoy an array of benefits. It is common for a community to have a "no-tipping" policy. Instead, residents are encouraged to contribute to an Employees' Appreciation Fund whose money is apportioned according to the number of hours worked. This way, all employees, whether seen or unseen by residents during their workdays, receive gratuities.

Every employee takes residents' concerns seriously, whether an issue is a complaint about debris in a stairwell or an alert that a dangerous crack has opened in a sidewalk.

Personal attention can happen in subtle ways. For instance, if a housekeeper should notice that a resident has declined noticeably in physical or mental ability, she is encouraged to report her concern to her supervisor, who alerts the Nurse or Social Worker, who then calls upon the resident to assess what may be happening in that resident's life.

A sign of a successful business is that everyone in the LPC – residents, staff, and employees – live and work in an atmosphere of care, compassion, camaraderie, living each day with an attitude of optimism. If this description sounds foolishly ideal, just wait. In your search for your own LPC home, you will visit at least one community where the staff and residents you meet are busy, fun-loving, independent, and secure. Clearly, an LPC is not just a business.

You get to know a community by means of your visits for tours and other events. For example, is there a Residents' Association or Residents' Council that meets regularly and has its own constitution and bylaws? Is the administration receptive to residents' proposals? Is it open to sharing details about finances and plans for improvements? What kind of feedback system is in place? Are open meetings between residents and administration scheduled multiple times a year?

Asking pointed questions like these will help you assess the relationship between administration and residents. Also, the community's Mission Statement may reveal how administrators shape their attitudes. For instance, one community's mission statement that it "cares for and enriches the lives of older adults, while valuing the staff, volunteers, and community that serve them."[18] This statement seems to place a balance among all who participate in the life of the community.

You want to feel that the planners of your community take their responsibility seriously:

A Social Commitment: In an ordinary real estate development, how we decide to design, build, and sell is a business decision. That is what home builders do all the time. Now, when we get to assisting the elderly and designing, building, and selling CCRCs [Continuing Care Retirement Communities], the program should change. It comes along with a very strong social commitment to provide for the community. And that can be done by either teaming up with an operating company or doing it ourselves, ….

What seniors are telling me, whether they are renting or buying in the facility, is that they are at the point in life where one of these days, they are going to need support. "I trust you to provide me with that support and [to] think through and manage the business necessities to provide this support. I trust you to select a nursing staff. I trust you to provide the type of long-term insurance I will need and fill out the paperwork on my behalf and make sure that they actually do what insurance policies are supposed to do in view of a constant flux of new laws, new regulations, new government, additions or subtractions from Medicare – it is getting be too much for me, and, as a senior, I cannot follow the laws that govern the insurance companies and

---

[18] Frederick Living Continuing Care Retirement Community, Frederick PA. https://frederickliving.org/about-us/core-values-mission/ accessed July 17, 2020.

implement the business action to offset them. By buying or renting in your facility, I will trust you to do all these things. I will trust that you have the vision to be there when I need you, which necessitates the commitment not to sell out after the first year." We have made a commitment internally in our family that we will not build and sell, we will build and operate to carry out the fiduciary and moral responsibility that we have taken on with these residents: service and good medical and financial security.[19]

Cook and Custodian: Gladys and Horace

After I asked Horace what he did before he retired, he enjoyed telling this story.

When our children were all in school, a neighbor told my wife Gladys there was an opening in the junior high cafeteria, so she applied and got the job. In six months or so, she was the manager. A few years later, when another junior high opened in the district and her principal was transferred to it, he asked her and a few others to transfer with him, so she became the first manager of that cafeteria.

In those days, everything was made from scratch – soup, meat, vegetables. She had a baker for cakes and pies. Around the holidays, sometimes a worker called in sick, but the work had to be done, so my wife set the alarm two hours earlier and at 5:00 AM she got up to help with the day's cooking.

I was first a custodian, then the head custodian, in another school in the district – I'd turned down that same job at my wife's

[19] Harrigan, John E., Jennifer M. Raiser, Phillip H. Raiser. *Senior Residences: Designing Retirement Communities for the Future.* John Wiley & Sons, Inc., NY. 1998. 60-61.

school on the advice of a friend who said it wouldn't look good for us both to be heading departments in the same building, but to tell the truth, we'd have made that school a real showplace!

Anyway, Gladys told me the cafeteria workers' toilet was broken and did I have a spare one to replace it? Well, I did have two extras, but I told her she should get the new one from her building's crew so their budget would pay for it. Nothing happened, and she asked me again, so I took one of my extra toilets over to her kitchen and installed it for them. About three days later, the Big Boss called. "Did you put one of your school's toilets into that other school?" "Yes, I did," I said. "Well, you've got to take it out. They must use their own budget." I pointed out some obvious other solutions, but he said I had to remove the toilet. I went back and took it out. Within a week, a couple of their guys showed up and, yep, they installed a new toilet. Go figure!

After my wife and I both retired, we stayed in our house for nearly twenty years, and we moved here ten years ago. Last year Gladys got sick and was in hospice care for her final months until she died just after Christmas. I'm a quiet guy who doesn't talk much, so I've enjoyed talking with you.

Marketing and Sales

The Marketing and Sales Department is a vital part of the LPC. Its job is to keep housing units filled, thereby providing the revenue that fuels the community. Compared to buying a second home or a vacation condo, buying an apartment or house in an LPC usually takes much more time. The salesperson must be patient, kind, and tenacious. Because prospective residents like to talk, the salesperson needs to be a good listener as well as outgoing, friendly, empathetic.

Your salesperson will be possibly a man but often is a woman who may remind you of a daughter or granddaughter in the way they show interest in your reactions and opinions. The more they hear what you want and need, the better they can help you find your perfect home. They know that you do not want to be called *elderly* and you do not feel ready for a *nursing home*. They will show you how the community is an upbeat, active, lively place to live. They respect you for what you are: a person with interests, health issues, attitudes of your own, and wisdom and expertise accumulated over a lifetime.

The salesperson conducts an informal focus-group when they ask, for example, whether you would pay extra for granite counter-tops or glass shower-walls or decorative moldings on the walls. Your replies suggest what the market wants so that the community can provide it to future residents. Retaining a competitive edge in the market is vital. That's why, as a prospective resident, you matter. Your opinion is valued. In fact, after you move in, your input may no longer seem important because Marketing focuses on their new prospective residents.

Your salesperson will contact you to suggest you see new vacancies, invite you to upcoming sales events, and ask whether there is any other way they can help you. The sales team are likely to be full-time, well-trained workers who receive a salary plus commissions, and sometimes bonuses. They help each other by sharing responsibilities for their clients and taking each other's calls. Like car sales-persons, they meet you, walk you through the ownership process no matter how many months or years it may take, address your concerns, and remain at your side on the day you sign the papers and receive your keys.

The salespeople know they have two competitors. One is the other LPCs that are vying for your business. The other is your house.

Your house is filled with emotional ties and years of memories; you may believe that staying there is much less costly than moving to a retirement complex. Their job is to show you that life in an LPC can be good in ways you've not thought about. They remind you that the community offers a support system that most people do not realize they need. For example, they encourage you to notice details like the friendly relationships among residents, comfortable gathering spots scattered throughout the complex, relaxed atmosphere, cleanliness everywhere, attractive handrails along the corridors, grab-bars in restrooms and bathrooms, and wide doorways in all apartments.

Sensing hesitation, your salesperson may ask about your concerns. In one community, when the conversation turned to the client's being worried about his upcoming surgery, the salesperson invited him to come to their Skilled Nursing facility, at reduced charge, for his rehabilitation. In another community, learning that the couple was concerned that their backgrounds in higher education and their non-religious beliefs might be hindrances to making friends, the salesperson arranged a private luncheon with six residents with similar backgrounds during which the couple learned directly from fellow residents that they would indeed find many friends here.

Keeping an active waitlist is vital. Even when occupancy is high, the sales team always strives to have a new resident eager to move into a vacancy. If the community is building new apartments or houses, the sales team does active pre-sales for at least two years ahead of opening.

The salesperson is aware that people may have two views: perception and reality. Most prospective residents see themselves as independent, living endlessly, and forever healthy when in fact they recognize at some level the issues of aging and their own mortality. As a prospective, you may notice that your salesperson may not promote Assisted Living and Skilled Nursing in the community. Pro-spectives do not want to think about the "nursing home" aspect of the community. However, your salesperson will welcome your in-quiries about nursing care services and will gladly accompany you on a personal tour of those wings if you request one.

Indeed, part of your final decision should be a visit to Assisted Living and Skilled Nursing. You can meet a few residents, observe their dining and activity rooms, notice the interactions among the staff and residents, and imagine how you might react if you or your spouse were living in that setting too.[20] After I toured the health care facilities at two different Communities, I came away thinking, "I hope I won't need to live there, but if I should, I think I'd be comfort-able." In fact, as the last part of my extensive evaluation, those ex-periences in Skilled Nursing sealed the deal: we submitted applica-tions to both communities.

Your salesperson's job is a delicate one. They want to close the sale yet also address each issue that is important to you, the client. For example, you may be an artist who wants your new work to be displayed within the community; may you do that? Or you may men-tion how uncomfortable you feel when you see walkers or wheel-chairs in the Dining Room; what new attitude would help you ad-dress this discomfort? Not infrequently, they need to acknowledge that one spouse doesn't want to think about a move while the other spouse is looking ahead to the benefits of living in a Life Plan Com-munity.

---

[20] From an LPC administrator: "I am so glad that you included the sugges-tion about visiting Assisted Care and Skilled Nursing. Many people avoid seeing what their future may hold, and I think that is a big mistake!"

Marketing vs. Sales

Have you wondered what the difference is between Marketing and Sales? You may develop a lengthy relationship with your salesperson yet never meet anyone on the marketing staff.

The salesperson has individual contact with prospective residents, has built up a clientele, is on good terms with residents and staff, and knows or finds the answers to your questions.

The marketing department creates brochures, advertisements, promotional events, direct mail, signs, media platforms, and websites. All promotional materials must be true and accurate, for the community is making promises to future residents that it is legally responsible to fulfill.

From your perspective, when you come away from a well-planned, lovely luncheon/tour event with a logo-embossed pen and 5x7 pad from the community, you appreciate both your salesperson who stays at your side and the marketing person who set up the event.

Does every community advertise? Some Communities have little need to promote their services because of robust resident referrals. Others run ads regularly, mount billboard displays, or have booths at community events. Best of all, word-of-mouth recommendations are sterling.

Some Marketing Departments encourage outsiders to hold events at the community. For example, the regional Horticultural Society may have its annual Flower Show in the auditorium, accompanied by food and snack service plus a bazaar; or an area Music Society may conduct its monthly meetings in a classroom, hosting a summer "thank you" concert in the auditorium for residents. Meanwhile, members of those groups are seeing what a lovely place this community is, with its inviting appearance, delicious food, and friendly helpful staff – some of whom may offer spontaneous tours of a vacant apartment, the library, and the pool and gym.

Members of the Marketing and Sales Department are eager to sell, but they are also honest and thoughtful about helping prospective residents enter an appropriate, happy new lifestyle.

Stay Positive!

Sitting in a conversation corner reading a book, I noticed a man approaching in a motorized wheelchair.

"Good morning," he said, "I see it's raining outside."

I agreed.

"It will end soon. We'll have sun by two o'clock. I've already put in my request."

"That'll be great," said I, and on he rolled, soon to do a U-turn and roll past again. "I'll return to celebrate the afternoon!" he said as he passed.

How easy it would be to feel bad for him, confined to a wheelchair. But this man banishes those glum feelings before they form. I don't know his name, but I look forward to meeting him again.

> Most folks are about as happy as they make up their minds to be.
>
> – Abraham Lincoln

I woke up this morning
determined to eat right and
exercise, but that was four hours
ago when I was younger and full
of hope.

7: Dining and Other Features

Questions: What may I want to know about food services? How do meal plans work? Which other services and amenities may be available at my Life Plan Community? How can I cope with so many choices?

Marketing and Sales focus on their dining services, especially the high quality of their restaurant-like fare. That is why a brunch or luncheon usually anchors the invitation to an Open House.

Most Life Plan Communities require a meal-plan of some sort, a "meal" being lunch, dinner and, in some communities, breakfast. Sometimes, you pay a fixed monthly amount for a set number of meals, with various ways to account for meals that you miss due to illness or travel. For example, you can use the value of missed meals by inviting friends or family members to dine with you as your guests.

Other communities offer flexible plans in which you pay in advance for a certain number of meals per month: ten, twenty, or thirty, for example. At every community, lunch and dinner menus can be substantial, so that someone who wanted just one hearty meal a day could choose either midday or evening. A few communities have no required meal-plan; for example, a wife or husband who loves to cook and wants to prepare all or most of the meals may prefer to use the dining room for only an occasional meal out.

Ambience is another dining consideration. I thought about the room I might want to eat in week after week. Do I thrive on table-linen, stemware, centerpieces, formal wait-staff, and dressy attire, or do I relax into the informality of placemats, tumblers, and casual clothes? I thought about Don's and my levels of interest: We both prefer simple, home-style cooking, few sauces, unadorned vegetables, healthy salads, few desserts, modest portions. Also, I considered our interest in cooking: not much. We would rather read a book or create a website than stand in the kitchen. Other people look forward to enjoying the Dining Room every day as a place to socialize, relax, and enjoy great food well served. Knowing what you really want can help you find the LPC that supplies it.

By participating in open-house brunches and lunches and by returning independently to sample lunch or dinner in the dining rooms of the communities we liked, we concluded that we preferred having no meal-plan required. With *à la carte* dining, we could order and pay for only what we wanted.

What a happy surprise that Rolling Meadow offered meal-plan options that included "none." In fact, after moving, we developed a delicious routine: Breakfast of cereal, fruit, coffee, milk enjoyed in the sunroom overlooking the hillside beneath an ever-changing sky. Light lunch of cheese 'n crackers, fruit, nuts, gingersnaps, served on paper plates with iced tea or water, shared in the living room while vying with contestants on recorded episodes of *Jeopardy*. And dinner, ah, a lovely dinner with friends.

Dinner *à la carte* in the Dining Room offers soup or salad; a tasty entrée such as chicken marsala, salmon Mediterranean, apricot ham, Hawaiian pizza, stuffed green peppers, chicken potpie; prime rib roast, pan seared scallops, stuffed pork loin; mashed or oven-roasted potatoes; vegetables, steamed and unseasoned; bread, biscuits, or rolls. Desserts include homemade pie, cake, cobbler, pudding as well as ice cream, cookies, sometimes tiramisu; and beverages, such as tea, coffee, ginger ale, cola, lemonade. We love the casual ambiance of the Dining Room. Servers know us by name, even greet us with the beverages they know we want. We ask about their lives and sometimes invite them to share a conservational joke that may be happening just then at our table.

Even more, we find that most of our friends are people we first met in the Dining Room. "May I sit with you?" and "Are these seats taken?" are common phrases as newcomers join a table. Words flow, banter abounds, world problems are solved, and an hour later, we're refreshed in body and renewed in spirit.

Dining out while dining in can be gentle on the pocketbook. Don totaled the receipts for six months in the Dining Room plus grocery store plus outside restaurants. Then he totaled the receipts for grocery and restaurants for a six-month period before we moved. The tallies were surprisingly similar. We realized we could enjoy good food with friends in a pleasant, relaxed setting at a cost similar to before we moved. And did I mention the joy of no cooking and no cleanup?

"Alcohol Allowed?"

One evening at dinner, I noticed a bottle of red wine atop a nearby table in the Dining Room. Until a few years ago, Rolling Meadow had been a dry campus. Then new residents revived discussions about allowing wine, beer, and even liquor on the premises.

One woman insisted that wine was unchristian. She declared that Jesus accepted wine only because, since the water wasn't healthy to drink, he had to convert it into wine. However, she was taken aback when a newcomer pointed out, "Couldn't Jesus just have purified the water?"

Another resident got permission to circumvent the no-alcohol rule. Apparently, his doctor had succumbed to the patient's argument that cited an old belief: nine golden raisins soaked in gin, taken daily, can reduce the pain of arthritis. A doctor's note was submitted. Once this unusual medication was approved, the man seemed to find that, if he partook of his marinated raisins every few hours, he felt better all day long.

I was dubious too, but subsequently I noticed this Letter to the Editor: "Lane offers a comprehensive look at the worldwide love of gin, but he leaves out one particular use of the spirit: folklore says that a regimen of nine gin-soaked golden raisins per day relieves arthritis pain almost as effectively as over-the-counter medications. Some have theorized that the juniper berries in gin combine potently with a substance in the raisins. Others say that any pain relief is due to the placebo effect. And still others maintain that straight gin will do the trick, no raisins required. John Huxhold Manchester, Mo." [21]

Finally, keeping up with the times, alcohol was permitted. It must be taken in moderation, provided by residents for their own use, and imbibed discreetly. Enjoying a bottle of wine with dinner became acceptable, but one mustn't draw attention to it. Residents are happy with this flexible policy.

Inside an LPC: Dining Services

The food industry is a major presence in retirement communities. From a national corporate level, contract foodservice companies often supply the structure, resources, and training that underlie what

---

[21] "The Mail," *The New Yorker*. December 30, 2019.

they call outstanding dining experiences at the local level. Their job is to provide excellence in dining, nutrition, and wellness. That is, their offers range from fine cuisine to homestyle favorites enjoyed in dining rooms, cafés, and pub settings; they feature fresh whole foods, often from local providers, made from scratch; and they feature the attention given to salt and calorie levels, lean and tender meats, healthy fats, high fiber, and probiotic awareness. As a result, meals are wholesome and delicious as well as attractive to the eye. For example,

> A lunch menu may include Manhattan clam chowder; Open-face roast beef sandwich (or) Cobb salad; mashed potatoes, onion rings, baby carrots; dessert of the day: Apple Crisp.

> A dinner menu may include Roasted tomato bisque; Herb-roasted salmon (or) Boneless breaded pork chop; mashed potatoes, wild rice, sautéed spinach, broccoli & cauliflower; dessert of the day: Piña Colada Cake.

Cura Hospitality,[22] one of many national food service companies available to LPCs, divides its business into these categories whose names illustrate the scope of their service:

- o   Events and Catering
- o   Food Service Management
- o   Culinary Leadership; Nutrition and Dietetics
- o   "Front of the House"
- o   "Back of the House"

---

[22] www.CuraHospitality.com

Available near the dining room is a three-ring binder whose pages detail the nutritional content of the food served daily during the preceding three months.

The goal is that each meal becomes an experience. The kitchen staff welcomes ideas and shares recipes across the company. The "Chef's Special" that appears many days each week gives the chef a chance to come up with something new or different; if residents love the dish, the recipe goes to headquarters for consideration, perhaps to join a master-file of excellent entrees for all Communities.

Another goal is to reduce food waste. For example, in commercial kitchens in the United States, "about 30 to 40 percent of food is unnecessarily wasted. This food is thrown out because it looks weird, it was not eaten during a meal, or it was unused and began to rot."[23] In contrast, the Dining Services manager in my community reports that her kitchen keeps food waste to just five percent; further, all vegetable waste is taken to the residents' community garden for their compost system. In other communities, chefs sometimes supervise their own kitchen gardens that produce vegetables and herbs in season, or local farmers supply fresh, home-grown chicken, pork, beef, vegetables, herbs, and fruit. Dining services set high standards for freshness, wholesomeness, and prudence.

A large company like Cura Hospitality employs twenty thousand workers in North America, one hundred thirty-two thousand across the world. Within each community, the food service manager hires local assistant cooks, kitchen helpers, and dining servers, sometimes providing high schoolers their first jobs.

---

[23] Shaw, Jim. "How to Minimize Food Waste in Commercial Kitchens: Try these tips to cut unnecessary expenses and help the environment," April 2017. https://www.fsrmagazine.com/expert-takes/how-minimize-food-waste-commercial-kitchens, accessed July 11, 2020.

The community offers themed meals throughout the year: for example, a traditional Easter dinner features ham, duck, and trout, pineapple stuffing, fresh green beans, and pecan pie; a western-style barbeque offers burgers, ribs, hot dogs, potato salad, honey-biscuits, corn on the cob, and strawberry shortcake; a Chinese buffet offers wonton soup, steamed dumplings, chicken with broccoli, shrimp with cashews, mini-eggrolls, fried rice, and of course fortune cookies.

In some communities, Dining Services also makes a part of their inventory available for purchase in a mini-mart or refrigerator-cabinet setting: for instance, milk, orange juice, eggs, freshly made salad bowls, entrees, soups, breads, cookies, cakes, pies, ice-cream sandwiches.

Like Marketing and Sales, Dining Services has huge importance in attracting new residents and in addressing not just the health but the happiness of current residents. The friendliness of the staff and the expertise of its leaders and chefs go far in promoting the comfort, safety, and security of the community.

First Date: Nick and Ina

At dinner one day, the newcomer asked, "How did you two meet?" Smiling, Ina spoke up:

I was in my thirties and getting a little bored with teaching, so I decided to take a graduate class one evening a week. My friend Kay was there too. I was a music teacher; she was a fourth-grade teacher. Nick was in our class, along with another man, Ken. The four of us got to know each other well enough that, when Nick and Ken completed their degrees, we celebrated together.

I had paid attention to Nick. I decided that Nick would be the perfect husband for ... Kay. I thought they'd make a great couple

91

and encouraged them to get to know each other better. They had a few dates, I think. But what I hadn't known about Kay was that she had a gentleman friend back in Wisconsin working on his graduate degree, and she planned to marry him and return to Wisconsin to live near both sets of their parents. Kay said she liked Nick well enough, but he wasn't the one. "That's too bad," I thought, and then let it go.

About a year and a half later, Nick and I happened to meet in the supermarket. I was buying ingredients, "and I was buying dinner!" added Nick. "I said, 'Good evening, Miss Cachia.'" Ina resumed the tale, "and I said, 'Hello'... and tried to remember his name!" We chatted a while and then went on our ways.

A few weeks later, Kay phoned me. "I want to tell you that I've given your contact information to Nick. He asked me about it, and I thought you wouldn't mind. But I do want you to know."

Well, late one afternoon a few weeks after that, I was planning to visit a young man in the hospital. He was my brother's friend from a town about twenty-five miles away, and my brother couldn't drive to see him very often. At that time, I had long hair, and on that evening, it looked a mess. The easiest thing to do was to pin it on top of my head and wear the short red wig that I'd bought for a lark at a time when I'd wondered how I'd look in short hair. I'd just checked my appearance when the doorbell rang.

"Who's that?" I thought. I wasn't expecting anyone. I opened the door, and it was Nick! He'd come over to renew our acquaintance. I don't know which of us was more surprised – me to see him, or him to see my short red hair!

"You know," said Nick, "I think it was that chance meeting in the market that got me thinking again about Ina. I'd become a

thirty-something Confirmed Old Bachelor, and I'd just about ex-pected never to meet the right person for me. It's an odd set of circumstances that brought us together. And that was over forty years ago."

Three pillars support your successful choice of a Life Plan Com-munity: Management, Marketing, and Meals. When they each per-form at an excellent level, you have found an outstanding commu-nity worthy of your consideration.

Checklists for Self-Assessment

After your visits to Life Plan Communities, you may want a chart to help recall where you went, what you saw, how you reacted, and other comments. Because the following charts are quite detailed, use only the items that interest you. Later, your checklist will help you to compare the communities you liked. Studying your impressions, you will find that your preferences for your new home will emerge as if from a mirage.

Checklist 1 – Basic Information for Each Community

Date: Your initial visit
Name: Formal name of this community
Address: Street and town/city location. Useful for mapping as well
    as mailing.
Locale: (urban, suburban, semi-rural, rural)
Website: Bookmark the community's website. Abundant infor-
    mation at your fingertips.
Contact Person: Salesperson and/or any other key persons who as-
    sist you.
Phone Number:
Email Address:
Mission Statement:
Current occupancy rate: (%)

Independent Living: (90% + is very good)
Assisted Living: (the higher, the better)
Nursing Care: (the higher, the better)
Other visit dates:
Dates of Application/Acceptance:
Wait-List Perks: Some communities give privileges such as
    Wellness Center, Events, Dinners.
Position on wait list: You may be told where you are ("#12") or
    given an estimate ("about six months").
Estimated Availability:
Date LPC was established:
Ownership:
Housing Divisions and Number of Units:
Independent Living apartments, cottages/villas:
Assisted Living:
Memory Care (dementia):
Skilled Nursing (Nursing Care):
Other: Guest apartments
        Respite Care
        Adult Day-Care
        Senior Affordable Housing
Contracts and Costs: for _____ (type of unit) with
    (single) (double) occupancy
Entry Fee: Type A (Life Care) $_____
or Type C (Fee-for Service) $_____
Refund range: in percentage - May go from 0% to 90%.
Monthly Fee: current
Average annual increase: over last ___ years was ____%
Pets allowed: no? yes? restrictions? fees?
Dining Services Management: Community? Company name?
Meal-plan options: #meals/month? Cost?
First impressions: attractive décor? welcoming atmosphere?
Dining Room: formal or informal; reservations or open seating
Café/Bistro:
Coffee/Snack-Bar:

Private Dining-Room: *(for family or small group)*
Outdoor/Patio Dining:
Mini-Mart:
Meals served daily: Breakfast? Lunch? Dinner?
Take-out available:
Delivery available: Fee?
Catering available:
Alcohol policy:
Special events: themed dinners, dessert socials, cocktail hours, etc.

No community has every option. Part of your walk-through is to see what appeals to you and to identify facilities you are likely to use. Keep in mind that you are paying for all the features of your community: some, you will appreciate as treats and adventures, but if you see others as extravagant or extraneous, you may be annoyed that your money is supporting them. For example, you may notice a promotion for a semi-annual, eight-course gourmet dinner with international wines, but you know you'd not participate. Or maybe you'd love it!

Checklist 2 – Housing Choices in Independent Living

Apartments: studio / 1-bedroom / 2-bedroom / 2-bedroom + den. patio or balcony?
Adjoined cottages/villas: 1 bedroom / 2-bedroom / 2-bedroom + den. patio? sunroom? garage?
Houses: 1-bedroom / 2-bedroom / 2-bedroom + den. patio? sunroom? garage?
Housing Services and Features:
    In-home housekeeping: Included? Fee?
    Linens: Provided? Fee?
    Utilities: *(gas, electric, water, sewage, trash)*
    Cable TV: *(Basic / Premium)*
    Telephone: *(Basic)*
    Wi-Fi:

Appliances: *(refrigerator, range/oven, garbage disposal, dishwasher, microwave, washer-dryer)*
Bathrooms: *1 full bath / 2 full baths / powder room*
Bathroom features: *tub/shower, single/double sink, exhaust fan, heat lamp, emergency call*
Gas fireplace:
Walk-in closet:
Built-in wall safe:
Wet bar:

Many Choices

On your tours of various Communities, you will see a variety of housing units, from apartments to adjoined cottages and even houses. With so much to choose from, you must think about three essentials: What do I need? What do I want? What can I pay for? If the community accepts your application, then you can choose your home to reflect your own wants, needs, and resources. Each visit to a community helps you to define what suits you and your lifestyle. It is a chance to assess, to dream, to focus, and to choose. And, oh, there may be many choices!

Each type of housing has its pros and cons. A big decision is Apartment versus House? For example, an apartment puts you at the center of activities and facilities. You can walk to where you want to go, convenient in time and weather. A villa/cottage (single, duplex, triplex, quadraplex, etc.) places you in a mini-neighborhood with streets, driveways, and possibly an attached garage and a private garden, but you may need to use your car, bicycle, or community transportation to attend events and to use Dining Services. In a house, you pay for most utilities but usually not for a meal-plan.

Your apartment or house can be small, medium, or large. Floor plans may vary such that two similar-sounding units may vary in arrangement of rooms, dimensions, even number of windows. If you want two bedrooms, would you like them adjacent or at opposite ends; two full bathrooms, or a bath and a half, or two and a half bathrooms? Entry foyer? Large versus small kitchen? What about the sun? Would you prefer a southern exposure with sunshine pouring through the room to brighten your day, or a northern exposure so you can disregard the need for pulling the shades or drawing the curtains? Would you prefer an upper floor versus lower? Near the elevator? (One woman asked for her apartment to be as far as possible from the Dining Room so that she would have to walk that distance daily, figuring she would get her exercise that way.)

The more apartments, cottages, and houses you visit, the more you discern what will be best for you. Meanwhile, during your visits, you will become acquainted with some of the many services that the community provides. Even though the following list is long, you may need to make additions.

> **Happiness, not in another place but in this place,**
> **Not for another hour but this hour.**
>
> **– Walt Whitman**

Checklist 3 – Services within the Community

Housekeeping:

Building maintenance:

Emergencies: Building or Apartment Problem

Fire Safety: fire-drills? / frequency?

Emergency Medical Devices:

Security: gate & guard at entry, sign-in at entry, open campus; exterior doors locked/unlocked

Receptionist and Hours:

Notary Service:

Fax machine:

Bank branch or ATM:

Hair care: beauty salon, nail salon, barber shop

Laundry service: self-serve laundry rooms

Trash/recycling/shredding rooms:

Transportation service: on-property / off-property; fee structure

Guest suite:

IT service: (computer, phone, and smart TV assistance)

Spiritual support:

Medical Clinic:

Delivery service: mail / packages / newspapers

Social Worker:

Move-in Coordinator:

Other(s):

As you tour, ask questions, even little ones. One afternoon, as the group passed a door marked "Trash/Recycling," I asked our tour leader how often the trash was collected. Expecting her to say, "Every other day," I was taken aback when she replied, "Twice a day." Now that I live here, I affirm that twice-daily pickups are necessary! On an open-house tour of several residents' apartments, I noticed how useful the kitchen island is, and inquired about it. I learned that during your apartment's renovation before you move in, a lovely, bi-level island can be permanently installed, or you can purchase your own island or simply put a small table and chairs in that spot.

From the time you sign your contract until you arrive, the Move-In Coordinator is your guide. With her, you discuss renovations to your new house or apartment. Most renovations are included in the contract: new appliances; cabinets in kitchen and bath; floor-coverings, paint, and decorative trim. Other "customized" features that a future resident may want, such as built-in bookshelves or desk, a sound system, or a TV-jack in the bathroom, may be installed at cost. Depending on the item, you may have to pay for installation now and then pay for removal later. These kinds of issues are under the guidance of your Salesperson or Move-In Coordinator. She may also provide advice or services to help you sell your house, find a mover, and even recommend agencies that pack and then unpack your boxes. What is replaced or included with a new move-in will vary from community to community. Policies regarding "who pays" will also vary. Be sure to ask.

Spotting "a Certain Something"

A particular feature in a community may capture attention: perhaps a tennis court, a lovely chapel, an intimate café, a fireplace flaming its warm invitation to sit awhile. What caught my eye the first time I visited Rolling Meadow was the mural in a four-story atrium. I looked up and saw a curved translucent skylight diffusing light all the way to the bottom floor; I looked down and saw three sleek koi gliding in a quiet pond. The sapphire blue mural with patches of green and touches of white expanded like an imaginative jungle-to-sky riverbed. Continuing the tour, I thought I saw the mural again, but this time at its bottom were lush plants with decorative rocks. At first, I mistrusted my memory. Then I realized there were *two* stunning, floor-to-skylight thirty-foot-high murals.

Two years later, when I supervised the arrival of my furniture into my top-floor apartment that overlooks an atrium, a moving man kept peering at the mural and its vista below. Finally, he caught my eye, and said, "I love this painting! I'd call it *Earth*." Ever since, *Earth* is what I call it too. This atrium opposite my apartment door has become my quiet place. Two comfortably cushioned rattan chairs and a matching sofa invite me there to read, think, chat with a passerby, and imagine a vast universe or a jungle or unexplored river trails.

You know you're getting old
when everything hurts and what
doesn't hurt doesn't work.

Interlude 1: Stories of Work Life

Your retirement community abounds with interesting people. That's why, for many residents, social interaction is the highlight of community living. Meeting others in casual ways can start a comfortable friendship. Learning about other people is fun.

What follows is the first of three *Interludes* relating anecdotes that represent what attentive ears heard at leisure. Beyond mere facts, residents' tales bring to life some of the treasures of community living.

George Eastman said his development of inexpensive photography gave the masses "the luxury of thinking about memories."[24] The luxury of memories happens almost daily over a meal in the Dining Room, coffee in a conversational corner, or visiting in a hillside gazebo. People enjoy telling stories – and listeners gain insights of their own. As their tales unfold, oh, how the speakers' eyes brighten. All you need to say is, "Tell me about what you did before you moved here."

---

[24] *"Kodak Misses Its Moment"* in *Spectacular Failures,* podcast, *Stitcher,* accessed July 24, 2019.

Perseverance: Eustacia

I was born on a little dairy farm in a tiny town in northern New Hampshire, north of Lake Winnipesaukee. My town was on a river, the Pemigewasset River that ran straight north-south and right through the center of town. Back in that day, the river was lined on both sides with paper mills. Lots of lumbermen were cutting vast acres of timber to send to those pulp mills. The chemical smell was distinctive, with the emphasis on "stink"! Someone said the odor was like cabbage simmering in a pot all day long – thinking about it that way made it kind of tolerable.

My father was deaf, so working with his small herd of twenty-five cows was a job he was suited to. He did all the milking, and my mother strained the milk and bottled it. Early each morning, my dad hitched the horse to the delivery wagon and made the rounds to his customers.

Sometimes he let me go along with him, and the ride was companionable. I helped when I could – I'd run the milk up to the back porches sometimes. I didn't have to go, but I thought I was special when he asked me along.

Now and then, at the end of the run, he'd stop at the general store and treat me to a candy bar. In those days, that really was a treat, and being a little girl, I always wanted that candy all to myself. I made sure to chomp it down fast before we got home where I'd have to share anything that was left. I remind myself now that at my age then, I was acting not nobly but, I'm embarrassed to say, naturally.

My parents worked hard. They had important jobs to do every day, seven days a week. Caring for the cows, providing fresh wholesome milk, running a household, and managing a family took stamina and dedication. I guess they had a routine, which made their tasks move along, but looking back, I can tell their work never ended.

I had three sisters, and our dad never made us labor. But sometimes he'd explain what he had to do, and what else also had to be done, and he'd ask if we could help. I remember carrying a bag and shovel along a path near the house and picking up the plops of cow manure that didn't belong there.

I went to the local school, then to college where I studied science. I worked as a microbiologist until a local school superintendent said he'd love me to teach in one of his elementary schools. Somehow, twenty-five years later, I was retiring from that classroom job I loved. I'm still in touch with some of my students from long ago.

Teaching: Gwendolyn

Gwendolyn remembered a class of high school seniors who thought she was too tough on them. In the Dining Room, leaning back in her chair, she sipped her decaf with dessert and continued:

In my classroom, the kids seemed to know which other classes I was teaching too, maybe from the bulletin board displays or the homework assignments I posted daily on the chalkboard. At the start of class one day, I was describing the work we'd be doing that week when an earnest voice protested: "Mrs. R., you treat us like an honors class!" Startled but realizing this boy represented the feeling they all had, I paused a moment and changed gears.

"Well," I said, "why wouldn't I make you work hard? You're just as smart as they are!" I'm sure they never expected that reply. This class of seventeen- and eighteen-year-olds was grouped as "general level" – students who aspired just to graduate and then go to trade schools, military, or local hourly jobs. I may have been the first educator to have ever told them they were as smart as the academic students.

Seizing the moment, I went on: "The only difference between you and honors kids is that they care about studying hard and getting into good colleges whereas you have other goals. School is important to them while to you school is something you go through on your way to something else you'd rather do. There's nothing I ask of the honors kids that you couldn't do, too, if you wanted to."

Silence suffused the room. These teenagers heard more than my sincerity: they heard respect. They heard their teacher articulate their attitudes, their goals, their capabilities, their choices. They heard a precursor of a thoughtful boss who might say, "This job assignment I want you to do is tough, but I think you can do it."

I've always been glad for that student's protest, for it let me open for him and his classmates a hidden window of insight: high expectations were right for them, and they themselves could take charge of their own potential in life.

Weight Watchers: Lorna

Neighbors in the hallway had gathered for a pot-luck supper, an event seasoned with plenty of lively conversation. Lorna had just said, "I couldn't go because I was lecturing that night...," and Delia leaned over to ask what kind of lecturing Lorna had done. Sitting straighter in her chair, animated by the memory, Lorna reminisced:

I used to lecture for Weight Watchers. Before that, when I was thirty-eight or so and had lost a hundred pounds, I had joined the

"One Hundred Club." Yes, I kept it off, too. I felt a lot better after I learned how to prepare my meals using Weight Watchers' recipes. If my children didn't like the main course for the evening meal, I cooked them what they wanted – mac 'n cheese, burgers, and so on. The family didn't mind my love of healthy cooking.

One day, I got a phone call from the president of the area Weight Watchers program. She invited me to her home, one of those big houses near the city. I didn't know why she'd invited me, so I was really surprised when she offered me a job. She wanted me to give talks to Weight Watchers groups. "What? Why me?" I asked her. "I don't have any training. I didn't even graduate from high school."

I guess she saw more in me than I ever did!

I ended up giving lectures all over the area – this town, that town, evening schools, halls. I'd drive twenty or more miles just to get to the places. My pay varied according to how many people attended, and that worked out okay because I often had fifty or more, even a hundred occasionally.

Sometimes I spoke in schools, lecturing children about nutrition. I taught an adult evening-school class that was very popular. The students paid twenty dollars for the eight-week cooking class. From that money I bought all the groceries and planned the menus. Each week in class, I showed how to prepare the dishes for that meal and supervised while they cooked. Then we all sat down and enjoyed the meal. That was a pretty good deal for them, wasn't it! Twenty dollars for eight meals. And I got paid, too.

When I started working for Weight Watchers, I was forty, and after twenty-six years, I decided it was time to stop. There were other things I wanted to do. At times I was working two jobs, and

I had outside interests as well. Meanwhile, my children were growing up and marrying and getting on with their own lives.

I told my husband I'd cook anything he wanted to eat, and then I'd make it using Weight Watchers recipes. Cheesecake? I'd use ricotta cheese instead of cream cheese. Pumpkin pie? Mine had a delicious filling with no crust underneath it. Whatever he wanted, I could make.

But after seven years, he told me he wanted his good old Pennsylvania Dutch food again – lots of potatoes, bread, meat 'n gravy, rich desserts. One of our neighbor ladies cooked old-style Pennsylvania Dutch – she even spoke Pennsylvania Dutch – and she shared her big meals with him. He had decided that, even if it cost him a few years of his life, he wanted to eat what he wanted to eat.

He kept on smoking too. He tried to stop, but after he died, I found out that when I was working, he'd sit in his chair in front of the television and smoke. When he'd see my car come up the driveway, he'd drop his cigarette into a little jar of water that he kept on the floor near his feet. My daughters told me this. They said they'd catch him smoking and tell him to stop, so I guess he ignored them too.

My friends said later, "Didn't you smell the smoke when you came in?" Well, in earlier years, he had smoked for so many years indoors that I thought I was just smelling the house! I never worked it out.

I figured he was an adult. He had a right to choose how he wanted to live. I guess that means he had a right to choose how he wanted to die too. He's been gone now for over fifteen years.

That story was kind of bittersweet, and I have another sad one too. I used to offer "One Hundred Plus" classes. To be in them, you had to want to lose at least a hundred pounds. In one of them, a woman usually brought her two children. The boy was about eight and the girl was about five. The kids behaved well, and I guess they listened to the lectures too, because the boy really wanted to have some of the reward badges I gave out when people had hit their weight-loss goals. The badges looked like little shoes kicking away those pounds.

He told me he'd work for a badge. He promised he would clean out the cellar that week, and he did it, and I gave him a badge. He said he would make his bed every day, and he did, and I gave him a badge. He was full of ways to help at home to get more badges. I probably shouldn't have given them to him, but I enjoyed his eagerness.

That year, the mother had a baby, and she brought the baby too, along with the other children. One evening, it was snowing outside, and she had to wait in line on the sidewalk to get in, so the baby had snowflakes on its hair. Meanwhile, the mother was complaining that something was wrong with her legs. It was like her muscles wouldn't do what they were supposed to do. I could tell that she was having trouble walking. She mentioned that she hoped she wouldn't have to use a wheelchair.

Soon after that, her husband got a job transfer and the family moved to Ohio somewhere. Later, I saw an awful headline in the newspaper – "Local family suffers loss in Ohio fire." It was that family! The husband had been at work when their house caught on fire. The two older children had been able to dash outside, and they survived. But the mother wouldn't leave without the baby, and the struggle to get him and then get out was too much for her. They both died in the fire. It was terrible.

After I left my job, they called me many times to come back or to fill in and give lectures. I really liked my work – meeting all those people, planning events, seeing how people changed. But Weight Watchers itself had changed, and I didn't want to teach their new philosophy. They were showing how you could eat sweet treats and desserts and not gain weight, but I really preferred the former instruction about cooking wholesome food in low-calorie ways. I didn't return. I had plenty of other ways to use my time.

Receptionist: Lillian

Lillian missed Monday's yoga class because at her church she takes her turn one Monday a month in a group that counts and allocates Sunday's collections of food and money. Totaling what came in during each of the four masses, filling out bank deposits, dividing food donations, and doing everything correctly, takes the group the whole morning. "They probably asked me because I used to work in a bank," she reflected, and then, thinking back to those days, she reminisced:

I was a teller for over thirty years. I was married then, and my husband and I had a little girl. I used to make all her clothes – once, I made a matching coat and hat for her. My sisters were all bigger than I, and when they gave me the clothes they'd grown too large for, I altered them to fit me. Some of those garments were expensive, too!

I retired from the bank. A while later, my husband died, and since I was financially secure, I didn't have to work. But the winters were long, and I became bored being home with little to do, so I thought I'd look for a job.

One day I drove past a nursing home and noticed a sign saying, "Receptionist Wanted." I wondered about it but drove on by. Three months later, the same sign was outside again. "Well," I thought, "that work could be interesting, even though I've never been a receptionist." I made a U-turn and went back.

When I met Betty, the woman in charge, I was direct: "Why can't you keep a receptionist?" was my greeting. That's unconventional, but she laughed in a friendly way.

She confided, "Well, we hire a young woman, and after a little while, when she finds out she must work weekends sometimes, she stops coming. She doesn't even call – she just doesn't show up. It's happened before, too. Why do you ask? Are you interested in the job?"

I filled in an application and gave my driver's license to be copied, and, since my wallet held my bank association card from my years as a teller, I gave them that too. A few days later, a man called me. "We like your application," he said, "but we have a concern about your age."

Here it comes, I thought. I'm in my seventies, and he's going to say I'm too old.

He went on. "We were surprised. From meeting you, Betty thought you were not much past middle age. But if you'd like to give it a try, we'd like to have you join us."

So, there I was, employed part-time in a friendly, helpful place where I could make a contribution. If a resident needed a little help or a friendly smile, I gave it, and I made sure always to keep busy doing meaningful work – no magazines, no phone calls with friends. I was their receptionist for eleven years and enjoyed it.

But then, after I met Enoch – he was eighty-four and lively, I was eighty-two – we were talking about getting married. He encouraged me to give up the job. I didn't really need the money, and he thought we'd enjoy doing things together and taking trips.

After our wedding, we combined our households, sold first one and then the other house, and moved here. Now we travel, take classes, go to social events, and do what we enjoy. Looking back, it's all good.

*I had so much fun at the pool that
I'm going back today!*

8: Making the Decision

Questions: What does the application involve? Why should I apply long before I decide to move? What are advantages of being on "the list"? Why should I revisit the community and take walks in the buildings and around its campus?

Application

Visiting many communities helped Don and me define that we wanted the following:

1. an apartment rather than a house,
2. in a community with levels of care,
3. with a fee-for-service financial structure,
4. located within eight miles of our daughters.

Of the eight Life Plan Communities I visited, four fulfilled our criteria for location, size, finances, cost, and ambience. We revisited those four LPCs for additional Open Houses, tours, and Q&As.

Don was mildly interested, saying he wasn't ready to think about it. However, when we visited Rolling Meadow, the last place on our list, he perked up. Returning to the car, he commented:

"I *like* this place."
"Why?" I asked.

"Because the whole thing is under one roof – you could do a lot of indoor walking here. And it doesn't have long straight corridors – the halls have turns and angles that make the place seem smaller than it is. And I like the grounds."

Well, that was enough for me. Since I liked all four, and having put down deposits at two places that he was only tepid about, I said, "Let's apply here too," and he agreed. He was on board.

Applications require deposits: refundable sums of at least $1,000 plus an administrative, non-refundable fee of $100 -$200. All applications require financial details. When you apply, an admissions committee evaluates your numbers and, if you're accepted, your name goes on a waitlist. Otherwise, your deposit is returned.

Being on "the list" can be important. Regardless of how many vacancies it has, each retirement community has Open Houses to attract new residents so that its occupancy rate is as high as possible. As a future resident, you often wait your turn to get in: when you decide to move, you benefit from being at or near the top of the list so that, when you're ready to move, you can choose your "perfect" apartment. At that point, you can accept or decline an opening according to your preferences. If you decline, you keep your place on the list while you wait for what you want.[25]

Some Communities will tell you where you are on the list; others will not but may imply it when you visit. Being on the list puts you under no obligation to move to that community, but you establish

---

[25] Caution: You will not lose your spot on the list, but you may become "inactive" after saying "no" a number of times. You then must notify them when you are ready. Also, communities may have a "ready" list that they will go to when a unit is available. Thus, Sales will not always call the list in order.

your option to choose. In a sense, your modest, non-refundable administrative fee ensures that you have choices.

Don's and my application to Rolling Meadow was accepted. Since we both could envision moving here "maybe in three years," we attended every subsequent Open House and requested to tour every two-bedroom apartment even when it didn't match what we thought we wanted.

Just like other Communities that offer various perks to its wait-listers, Rolling Meadow encouraged us to use the Wellness Center as guests. What a great experience to attend aquacise classes once or twice a week for nearly a year. I not only exercised in the beautiful, heated swimming pool whose floor-to-ceiling glass wall overlooks a landscaped Courtyard, I also became friends with residents who awaited news: "Do you have an apartment yet?" "When will you be coming?" Socializing with them after class, I learned about trips, activities, the Grand Illumination Christmas fest when the Courtyard lights are switched on, movie nights, and the happily enjoyed Ice Cream Socials each third Wednesday of the month. Later, when we moved here, I already had five or six friends from the pool and looked forward to myriad activities to do.

Every couple of months, we came for a meal, including Thanksgiving Dinner. People looked at us, wondering who we were, and vice versa. Assuming we were new arrivals, people greeted us warmly. We walked through the halls to get to know the building. On official tours, I'd found it hard to keep my bearings – I felt like I was a mouse in a maze – so one day I carried the community floor plan to mark as we walked along. "Third floor *here*, library," I'd write. "Fifth floor *here*, mini mart. First floor *here*, recreation room. Fourth floor *here*, meeting room with tables. Top floor *here*, auditorium; underneath it *here*, dining room." As of that day, I understood how to navigate the building. Ah!

Lively Imagination

Do you know Eleanor Holman? Her father was on the board of directors for the big church summer camp across the road from here. She practically grew up there. I think her family had a cabin on the property, so they spent lots of spring and fall weekends and many full weeks of summer there. Anyway, when she needed to give up her house, she wanted to move to North Carolina to live with her son. He has a beautiful place there. It overlooks a lake and has a wide lawn that drops steeply down from the patio to the lake, with a drop right into shallow water.

Eleanor loved the house, the view, and especially her son and his family. But she has a lively mind, and her imagination got active. She worried that one day she'd be walking on the grass, fall, tumble down that slope, splash into the water, and drown! That image haunted her. Her solution was to come here to Rolling Meadow where she has a lifetime of friends and memories – and no chance of cascading into a lake.

Overheard in the Gift Shop

Meryl: My husband had a stroke last year, and afterwards he wanted to drive again. I told him he couldn't drive unless a driving-school teacher told him it'd be okay, and the doctor would have to approve too. Well, he didn't want to do that, so I'm the driver all the time.

Amy: My husband used to make local deliveries for a pharmacy – he knew all the back roads in this whole area. Then he started to get mixed up on his routes. One day I asked him how to get into town, and he couldn't remember, so now he's given up his license. It's safer this way.

Meryl: Well, that's how it goes sometimes.

Amy: Yep, it could be worse.

A Stroll around the Campus

On a balmy spring afternoon, a year before moving to Rolling Meadow, having noticed a macadam trail near the main entrance, Don and I explored the campus. Strolling along the one-mile walking path, we gained yet another perspective about our future lives here.

To our right, the extensive building, shaped in a giant horseshoe, covers a downward slope as does a split-level home so that the main entrance, at ground level, has a second floor beneath it with tall windows facing the Courtyard. Then, as the building expands down the hill, its floors increase in number from two to three to four and finally to five. A two-story bridge-corridor connects two of the buildings on floors four and five, and – outdoors – you can walk under the bridge to enter the large, landscaped Courtyard. This day, to explore the grounds, we stayed on the outer path.

To the left of the path, Don and I passed grassy areas with shrubs and flowers amid clusters of trees, some still boasting their early spring blooms. We walked around the residents' garden with its many raised beds, large well-tended compost pile, neatly coiled water hoses, and a red shed whose open door revealed folding chairs, wheelbarrows, and countless tools hanging on the walls. A comfortable sense of orderliness covered the garden.

Community Compost: Preston

Ten years ago, I thought of a plan to make compost by collecting food scraps from our residents. Because I was still working full time, the amount of work to implement my program was beyond my capacity. I wrote to residents to propose a volunteer composting plan in which people would bring their compost materials to the garden.

When we started, fifteen or twenty residents faithfully brought their produce scraps. To this day, Flora and I usually bring between five and ten pounds a week. A few years ago, I persuaded the dining room staff to contribute, so now a kitchen worker brings their fruit and vegetable scraps. During the summer when the chefs use a lot of fresh veggies and fruit, they bring a hundred or more pounds per week. Coupled with the leaves from fall cleanup, we have abundant compost materials.

My compost pile for next year is almost done, and then I will begin on the one for the following year. I have four large bins, one in use this year, and one for each of the next three years. They are 8'x8'x5'. It is amazing that vegetable matter, leaves, grass, and whatever biodegradable material that you put into a compost bin will give you rich black soil in two years.

Four compost bins. The one on the right is ready to fill for the future.

World-wide, composting has developed into a much bigger program that replenishes the earth. What we are doing at Rolling Meadow is a drop in the bucket, but if everyone composted at their level, we would have less material in landfills and better soil. My dad had a small compost pile, and it was absolutely the answer for fertile soil and a good harvest.

8: Making the Decision

The path near the garden overlooked a well-tended bocce court that we later learned was built by a Boy Scout as his Eagle Scout project. Nearby lay a large pond beneath a high pavilion with deck-chairs, picnic-tables, and two gas grills. Later, as residents, we saw, in season, Canada geese and mallard ducks browsing the pond and its banks. Occasionally, a statuesque blue heron arrives to peer into the water ready to strike a fish idling past. We learned that the pond is stocked so children can do catch-and-release fishing with Grandma and Grandpa. Turning left on the path, we walked past a gazebo and crossed a service-road to continue along a tree-lined creek. Walking across a footbridge, we passed a shady picnic area with tables and two pedestals supporting old-fashioned charcoal grills.

We encountered another fork in the path. To our left we looked upward across a sloping meadow that long ago had been a large pasture with a small stable. Atop the hill was another gazebo. Up we went along the path that meandered just enough to suit our speeding heartbeats, passing on our right a bench near a small, sheltered grove – for grandchildren, a secret fort.

Ascending to the hilltop gazebo, we surveyed the vista, gazing in one direction at the local hospital two miles distant and then straight across the property to the fifth floor of the community. Shrubs and flowering trees surrounded us. Chirping birds fluttered among weathered birdhouses attached to poles scattered over the meadow. Behind us and mostly hidden from view was an elementary school whose students, we learned, walk to the community in October in their Halloween costumes to trick-or-treat with residents in Assisted Living.

Sitting there, I envisioned that, after I move here, I'll visit this place often. Indeed, I do, sometimes bringing a coffee, snack, and book with me. As it happens, our apartment is direct line-of-sight from the hilltop gazebo, and now and then Don on the balcony waves to me while I wave back from my quiet hilltop retreat.

We returned to the fork and continued strolling along the circumference of the community. A zigzag wooden walkway led to a covered bridge that we learned later had originally been in use in Lancaster County PA. Its high railing invited us to examine the foliage, rocks, and rivulet a few feet below. What a peaceful setting.

On we went and, when the trail ended, we rejoined the sidewalk to complete our journey around the building. Benches dotted the trail. Having wandered our path of discovery for nearly an hour, we were ready to sit and rest in the warm sunshine, looking across a wide lawn toward the Skilled Nursing wing.

Soon, a long, low white vehicle arrived. It parked near a door. Two workers removed a stretcher, snapped its undercarriage wheels in place, and entered the building. Five minutes later, they returned with a shrouded figure lying on the gurney. Oh dear. A resident must have died, and these men were probably from the funeral home.

The sight rattled Don. "This is something I don't like," he reflected. "I know that people die, but I don't like knowing that we are coming here to die." His distress, and its frankness, concerned me.

"Perhaps there's another way to look at it," I said. "You and I are going to die too. The question is, *where* will we be, and *when* will it be? Right now, we're healthy and active, and we don't expect to die any time soon. What we can do is choose where we'd like to spend our final years before we're the ones the hearse is calling for."

"Yes," Don said, "but everyone here will be dying, and that's depressing."

I paused, then went on: "Everyone we know is going to die. That's a fact of life. We'll just have to be aware of keeping our focus on living a good life now while we can."

Sages tell us that acknowledging fear is important. I was glad that this unexpected occurrence opened an insight into our ultimate future no matter where we might be living, when first one and then the other one dies. But before then, we have the rest of our lives to enjoy.

A few minutes later, we continued our walk to its conclusion. In our journey, we had discovered beautiful outdoor features of Rolling Meadow and had confronted a reality of our final years: life is finite, live it where we'll be happy.

In adding "attractive campus" as an important criterion for our retirement community, we had discovered what turned out to be, for us, the most suitable Life Plan Community of all.

A Quiet Scene

From my top floor balcony on a warm, sunny day, I'm enjoying this low humidity, insect-free May afternoon. Below me the lawn is centered by an old evergreen whose lower branches struggle to keep their needles while the upper branches wave in the gentle breeze. A curved garden surrounds the tree. To its left is a smooth concrete path beyond which is "the basin," a watery, grass-filled catch-basin that manages the overflow when we have heavy rain.

Since late winter, red-winged blackbirds have occupied the basin and its surrounding grass, garden, and the tall conifer. High above the scene, in my shadowed recess, I can observe unnoticed. One neighbor, Kayla, has been tending the flowers she planted earlier in the month, carrying a small watering can back and forth from an outside tap. Meanwhile, Anita on the ground floor is tending her hanging baskets and potted plants on her patio. She grows flowers for beauty and herbs for her kitchen. She tends her three bird feeders, hummingbird sipper, and two hanging plants, one already loaded with pink blossoms. A wire grid stands empty at the side of her balcony – I imagine vines or creepers will grow into a leafy wall that adds charm to her mini-garden.

Look – Kayla is chatting with Anita, whose garden-gloved hands keep wielding her trowel, visiting like over-the-fence neighbors anywhere.

Since today is Tuesday, the landscapers are here. They seem choreographed. On the spacious meadow far to the left, three riding mowers swoop forth and back making wide ribbons on the grass.

Four other workers are mulching the shrubs and garden-beds, blowing soft black chips from a six-inch tube that stretches scores of yards across the lawns from a feeder truck. The handlers sway to and fro while walking slowly sideways to make a dark, even coating to last all the coming months through winter until this time next year. Smells suffuse the air – mulch is pungent, not quite manure, not unpleasant, full-bodied, earthy. Freshly cut grass, sweet and full, reminds me of childhood weekends when Dad was doing this same yardwork: trim, transplant, and care for grass, trees, and shrubs.

Machines roar at levels only a little less than annoying. When mulch-blowers and grass-cutters cut their engines and move on, then weed-whackers begin their melodious whines.

From my lofty perch, the crew and their boss labor continuously. I admire their work ethic: on task, industrious, great teamwork. On my Tuesday morning walks, whenever I give a wave and a thumbs-up sign to signal, "It looks great!" workers respond with friendly waves and smiles.

To me, our balcony is a treasure that affords fresh air, smells, and sounds, a mental escape from the confines of physical walls. From four o'clock Tuesday afternoon to the next Tuesday morning, my balcony is quiet, peaceful, private, serene; but in spring, summer, and fall on Tuesdays, it's a place of pastoral action.

Birds on the Meadow

I especially love the view from our top-floor apartment: My gaze rises above a line of parked cars to the vast hillside meadow beyond. I enjoy the peace while thinking my thoughts.

In late Fall and early Spring, migrating Canada geese take their rest on the hill. Leaders spotting the sunny, warm slope lead the descent. In flocks of twenty, forty, or more, they arc downward in unison, wings flapping vigorously, feet angled forward, throats honking, until they settle on the grass.

They gabble for minutes before quieting – until another flock appears, their eyes fixed on that cozy hill until they also swoop in, stretch down their legs, and land. Then a louder ruckus sounds out.

Each flock makes its own territory until someone thinks someone else is intruding, leading to a loud confrontation. Finally, the newcomers waddle away to a neutral space. Everyone settles down. Quiet blankets the hillside again.

Like Holden Caulfield who wondered where the ducks go in winter, concerned no doubt with who would take care of him in the harsh times of his life, I wondered where the geese rested on overcast days when they can't see the ground.

Then I considered the perspective of the geese aloft. Thousands of feet high, wings muscling their bodies toward their destination, trusting their leader who sets the course and then switches position with another leader to share the wind-flow burden, honking their airborne conversations so loudly I can hear them far below, they fly with confidence, determination, power.

Above or through the clouds that obscure my meadow, do they fly until they spot shafts of sun raying to the ground? There it is! Way over there! And look, a field! It's warm and practically empty. That's what we're looking for. That's where we're going!

An ornithologist can tell me what the geese do when rain pours for days or when masses of heavy clouds extend for hundreds of miles. In my mind, those instinct-driven, lofty, trusting birds prevail because they persist. Like Annie in the musical, they know the sun will come out tomorrow – if not here, somewhere; if not now, sometime.

> Happiness doesn't depend on any external conditions. It is governed by our mental attitude.
> – Dale Carnegie

9: Getting to Yes

Questions: What features do I want in my home? How does it feel to get the call? What happens after I accept an offer?

Identifying What You Want

Everyone has different values, needs, priorities. As I describe our reasoning, you can use it to develop your own criteria to answer the question, "What do I want?"

Because Don and I could take our time to select what we'd really like, choosing our apartment became a project. We had a goal but no need to hurry. We realized, however, that we had to be ready to accept an apartment within as few as twenty-four hours when the right one presented itself.

We liked Rhoda-Marie, our sales representative at Rolling Meadow. She was smart, lively, empathetic, focused, motivated. When we asked to see each two-bedroom apartment that became available, even when she and we knew we probably wouldn't want it, she agreed. She mentioned that, despite printed floor plans (studio, one-bedroom, two-bedroom), each apartment was different because of renovations over the years. For example, a two-bedroom might have a connecting bathroom ("Jack 'n Jill"), a bath and a half, or occasionally two full bathrooms. A bathroom might have a window, while most do not. A bedroom might have two windows, while most have just one. Some two-bedroom units have interior hall-ways, others do not.

Further, the more apartments we saw, the more we discerned what was important to us (for example, we wanted two full bath-rooms) versus what didn't matter (we didn't want a built-in kitchen island or an electric fireplace). Every apartment had a bright, inviting sunroom featuring floor-to-ceiling glass walls: We knew we wanted that feature.

We realized that apartments were in three connected buildings, each building a different age and each closer to or further from places like the Dining Room, Multi-Purpose Room, and the pool and exercise center. We learned that more recent (hence, younger) res-idents seemed to live in the newest building, but we decided that being the youngsters in an older neighborhood would be fine. We noticed that halls and meet-up areas were generally quiet, and both then and now, we rarely hear loud noises or smell food odors.

Everywhere we looked, we saw cleanliness, neatness, attentive-ness, signaling that this property was well maintained. Of im-portance, whenever we passed residents walking in the halls or working jigsaw puzzles, they looked us in the eye. People smiled, welcomed us, and encouraged us to move – "You'll love it here! We do!" We noted many small, attractive sitting areas that invited us to stop for a while and read or visit. All in all, the atmosphere was a curious mix of opposites – cozy yet spacious, inviting yet intimate. We felt at home long before we moved here.

We kept refining which elements would be important in our new home. For example, what about natural light: Which way would we prefer our apartment to face – full sun, partial sun, or no direct sun? Within the horseshoe shape of Independent Living, the beautiful Courtyard with ponds, paths, and pergola is generously bathed in sunlight from morning to evening, but direct sun pours into the tall windows of the surrounding apartments too. How hot are these apartments? And how bright? On the other hand, the outer-facing apartments that overlook trees, hillside, pond, and parking receive only limited direct sunlight. Would we yearn for some sunshine inside? What about the view? Choosing an exposure implied choosing a view, and we considered its importance too.

What about floor level? A ground-floor apartment exits onto a patio or grass, but its bathroom and kitchen might be subject to someone else's plumbing problem from above. A top-floor apartment might have a lofty view but requires waiting for the elevator or climbing flights of stairs.

For each option, pros and cons came to mind to consider and discuss. Don wanted the top floor (he dreaded the thought of water overflowing someone else's sink into our kitchen); I wanted limited direct sun so I could keep the windows free of curtains. He wanted plenty of office space. I wanted a spacious view of the sky. We agreed on many features: two full bathrooms (a "his" and a "hers"); two bedrooms (so that the larger one could be our office filled with computers, printer, files, desks, project supplies, and books); the sunroom; and our dream – not that we expected ever to have one – a balcony on which we could enjoy fresh air any time we wanted.

To get the features we wanted, we were prepared to wait a long time.

Yes!

Rhoda-Marie noted our wishes. The three of us understood that when the right place turned up, we would take it. Don was hoping for a three-year wait; I was expecting an eighteen-month wait; the reality was that our apartment showed up just six months later.

9: Getting to Yes

On a Thursday, Rhoda-Marie phoned: "I have a place that I think meets your criteria. When can you come to see it?" The next morning, she first took us through a fully furnished apartment whose footprint matched that of the new opening. We liked this apartment, for sure. Then, walking toward the available unit, Rhoda-Marie said, "We don't usually take prospectives through an apartment that's under construction, but another couple had taken it and then, after the renovation began, they withdrew their contract."

Quite a scene lay within.

Turning off their radio, two workers paused their drilling so we could tour the rooms. We had walked into a construction zone. All rooms were demolished to bare walls and concrete floor, for they were combining a one-bedroom unit with a studio to make a new two-bedroom apartment. To create a connecting doorway, a thick weight-bearing wall was being sledge-hammered, its edges still jagged with raw brick. Electrical conduit looped from the ceiling, bits of wood strips and wallboard littered the floor, an old bathtub stood alone in the middle of the living room, plaster dust and the odor of concrete suffused the air.

What a dynamic, glorious sight! Not for nothing had I played with Tinker Toys and Lincoln Logs when I was that little girl who loved to climb though half-built houses in a new development near my childhood home. On TV, *How It's Made* is a favorite.

Having just come from its attractively furnished twin across the hall, I had no trouble envisioning how we could settle into this space. My eyes sparkled; Don remained stoic. Thus, when Rhoda-Marie asked as she always did, "Well, what do you think of it?" I opined, "It's certainly high up for consideration." With her upbeat smile, she turned to Don who gave his usual reply: "I'm not ready yet."

9: Getting to Yes

Speaking pleasantries and a promise to call her Monday with an answer, we thanked Rhoda-Marie and headed for our car.

That evening, I commented that it was a terrific apartment that looked right for us. Don acted disinterested.

Saturday at 4:30 AM, I awoke wide-eyed, thinking about our quest. Three hours later, Don found me sitting on our porch with a coffee cup in hand and a serious expression. He said, "Did I do something wrong?" "Not at all," I replied, "but I think we need to talk." Oh no! I had uttered the Joan Rivers line that strikes fear into every man!

He was attentive and I was succinct: Rolling Meadow was the place we both liked a lot. This apartment met all our criteria – two bedrooms, two full bathrooms, large kitchen, top floor, lovely view, no direct sunlight, AND it even had what we never dreamed possible, an open-air balcony. "This apartment has everything we agreed we wanted," I concluded, "and if we don't take it, and later we move to another apartment, whenever we'd walk by this one, we'd be sorry we declined it." With this reasoning, our two logical minds united, and Don concurred: "Okay, let's tell Rhoda-Marie we'll take it."

But Monday morning, we learned that our saying yes did not conclude the deal. Oh no! It turned out that another couple was above us on the waitlist. They wanted a two-bedroom too, and therefore *our* apartment was theirs if they wanted it. What a disappointment.

Worse, the other couple was in the Bahamas and would return in another week. Unlike some communities which require a yes/no verbal reply within forty-eight hours' notice that an apartment was available to them, no matter where in the world they were, Rolling Meadow allowed prospective residents to tour the premises first. The protocol required us to wait a week for them to return.

In an email to my sister, I confided, "Many people decline apartments, so there's hope, but Don and I are assuming that this one may fall from our grasp, and we'll just to wait for another one like it, which may or may not happen."

As each day of that week crept by, we realized we really wanted this apartment. It suited us perfectly. I put my thinking-cap on. Knowing the other couple would be seeing it soon, I strove to find a diplomatic way to signal our strong desire to have this unit. By Sunday evening, I had composed an email for Rhoda-Marie to open first thing Monday morning:

> **Good morning, Rhoda Marie. If you're curious, or in case it's helpful, I can say that our level of interest in that apartment is very high. With hopefulness, we await word from you about the fate of "our" fifth floor apartment.**

I hoped that she wouldn't try too hard to sell this apartment to the other couple because, if they declined it, she had already sold it to us.

Phone Call

The next Monday, I held my breath, but alas, Rhoda-Marie was out of the office celebrating her birthday. Her voicemail said she'd be out on Tuesday too. Patience! I knew Wednesday was the day. Nothing else to do but keep calm and stay busy. We had already waited nine days – we could manage a few more hours. What other choice did we have?

Wednesday morning was hot and humid, as expected in August. I sorted books into piles labeled *Keep, Donate, Discard*. Don did yardwork ahead of the afternoon steam bath. Neither of us mentioned that this was the day the other couple would view the apartment.

Thus, when the phone rang at 10:45, we were both involved in distractions.

"Good morning," said Rhoda-Marie. Knowing she didn't need to identify herself, she sang out, "It's yours!"

"What?? It's ours? They didn't want it?"

"Yes," she said. "The wife liked it, but the husband said he wasn't ready to move yet – this was too soon."

"Wow! Wait – Don's cutting the grass – let me take the phone outside so you can tell him the news yourself. Is that okay?"

"Sure!"

Out the back door I flew and ran around to the side of the house. Seeing me with the phone, Don cut the engine. His sweatband was wet, his face slick with perspiration. Holding out the phone, I said, "It's Rhoda-Marie. She has an answer."

A huge smile suffused Don's face as he heard the good news. "Thanks so much for telling us," he said, handing the phone back to me.

"There's one more thing," I said to Rhoda-Marie. "This is happy news for another reason too – today is Don's birthday!"

The following email to friends and family describes our thoughts and what would happen next:

Don and I have accepted an apartment at Rolling Meadow. It's about as perfect for us as any we could hope to find, and we're optimistic about moving there.

The apartment has two bedrooms, two full bathrooms, a mid-size kitchen, sunroom, and balcony. It's on the top floor facing

west-northwest overlooking a landscaped basin, a wide up-sloping meadow, and a sweeping view for miles, from the top of this ridge over a valley to the Hilltop Hospital atop the next ridge. The setting is gorgeous: open, uplifting, contemplative. We may move early in November, perhaps sooner, who knows. We expect not to list the house until close to moving, and we hope to have about a month's overlap to make the move/sale easier on us.

We have begun the paperwork. First, medical approval. Then a wellness check by Rockhill's nurse and a mental check by the social worker. Then a financial check to confirm we have the dollars we said we did. Then the contract for our lawyer to read. Then a sit-me-down with the apartment coordinator to choose our paint, carpet, counter-tops, and decide about shower doors.

That'll all take two to three weeks. Then we must provide a five-figure deposit and sign the contract. About sixty days later, we'll take possession and start our monthly payments.

All in all, in approximately three months, certainly by Thanksgiving, we should be "in." [And that's what happened: we moved the first Tuesday in November, Election Day.]

We're well into downsizing, and what's left to do is manageable. Meanwhile, Don is not unhappy about giving up grass cutting, snow shoveling, and home repairs. We agree that now is the time to go.

The next four months saw us active every day, as expected. Five months later, well established in Rolling Meadow, I enjoyed this conversation about newcomers settling in:

How Many Bedrooms? Clara, Herb, Amy

At the coffee-station down the hall, where sofas and easy chairs invite visiting, Clara was filling two cups. Herb, Amy, and Clara were already chatting.

"There's a sales event today. That's odd because nearly all the apartments are filled," said Herb.

"They're adding to the waitlist, I suppose," said Amy.

"Yep, all the two-bedrooms are filled, and only three one-bedrooms are left."

"They never have enough two-bedrooms. Everyone wants them," said Herb. "Sometimes, you know, it takes a while for two people to adjust to a smaller apartment. You're kind of on top of each other 'til you get used to things."

"It was easy for us," Clara joined in. "Mark was so ill with his cancer that we had to move into the family room of our house so I could take care of him, and I didn't want to leave him alone any more than I had to. So, we got used to living in just the family room and kitchen. In a way, we expanded when we moved into our apartment here."

Herb added, "Remember that new couple who said they moved here after they realized they had a four-bedroom house but were living in only their bedroom, the living room, and the kitchen?"

Amy added, "My brother and his wife sold their house and lived for five years in one of those big RV's. They traveled all over the country. I always wondered how they managed to co-exist — she's a neatnik and he's a clutterbug. But they loved it."

Herb smiled: "Sometimes I think my wife nicknamed me 'Get Outta Here.' That's when it's time for me to take the dog for a walk. But we've been married sixty-three years, and we get along fine. Maybe I should rent out our second bedroom – but then I'd have to sleep in the car, and that wouldn't be much fun!" What an imagination, I thought.

I entered the recollections: "About three weeks after we moved here, Don acted testy, and I could tell he wanted to focus totally on his computer project with no interruptions from me. So, I took my book and coffee and disappeared to a reading corner in another hallway. Problem solved. Funnily enough, that never happened again. I guess when a couple is sensitive to each other's moods and is willing to make little adjustments, the apartment keeps its harmony."

We four split up – Clara carried her two coffee cups back to her apartment, I headed to mine with my insulated mug of iced coffee, and Herb and Amy stayed on the sofa awaiting the next imbibers looking for morning coffee 'n conversation.

Details, Details

Accepting the apartment involved paperwork and money. We submitted a financial update and a doctor's certificate of health. We signed a preliminary contract and handed over a check for several thousand dollars. We received a sheaf of forms to complete, and we made an appointment with the move-in coordinator to choose appliances, paint, and floor coverings plus other choices unique to our own apartment such as glass shower doors versus a traditional curtain-rod. During the following three months while renovations were being completed, we could visit the apartment by appointment.

A friend gave a valued suggestion: she said to make accurate measurements of each room and draw the apartment onto a large floor plan. I taped four 8½"x11" sheets of quarter-inch graph paper into a 17"x22" rectangle and lined out a true drawing of our new home. As well as the rooms, the diagram included doorways, window widths and heights, closets, and kitchen appliances and counters.

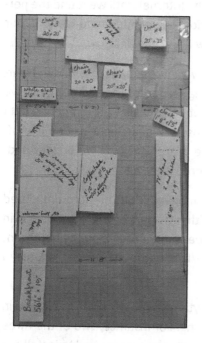

Floor plan mockups:

The sunroom is at the top, the living room in the middle, and the entry at the bottom, without kitchen appliances shown. Other drawings depicted the bedroom – bath – laundry and the office – bath – storage. These pages greatly helped us envision the apartment during the weeks before we moved.

Having measured the furniture we hoped to bring, I drew their shapes on graph paper, labeled them, and cut them out. That process took a week. It reminded me of paper-dolls or model-building: not easy but enjoyable. I arranged our furniture cut-outs on the 11"x17" apartment grid. Over subsequent weeks, Don added his ideas, and we considered sight-angles, walk-throughs, and what we needed versus what we wanted. Finally, we had a plan that satisfied us both. I photographed and printed each room's plan so that, on moving day, when Don was outside supervising the men at the truck, I could greet them at the door and say exactly where to place each item. What a help to their energy and to our checkbook, for we were paying them by the hour.

There were other benefits to using a detailed floor plan. Having declined the built-in kitchen island because we preferred a different, less expensive style, we scoured the Internet until we found the perfect island: We knew the dimensions we wanted, and we took our time to choose among quite a few attractive designs.

Knowing dimensions and views, we explored window treatments: we ordered room-darkening shades for the bedroom, and we realized we could delay thinking about curtains and draperies until after we moved in. Indeed, because our apartment has no line-of-sight neighbors, it was only three years later that we bought bedroom curtains, and we never ordered draperies.

A detail requested ahead of moving could be accommodated during the renovation process either as part of the work or for an agreed-upon cost. For example, we wanted timers on the bathroom fans and an additional ceiling fan/light centered above the kitchen island.

Alas, we failed to think of everything. We later discovered certain other details that required tweaking. For instance, two of the three pairs of sliding closet-doors were so heavy that we had to install our own handles; one tall kitchen cabinet had only the standard two shelves, but, having the space for, and needing, a third shelf, we ordered it ourselves from the cabinetry supply company. Our cost for one 10x30 inch matching plank was the princely sum of ninety dollars.

Well ahead of time, however, we had realized that the more we knew, the happier we would be. The sales team wanted us to move into an apartment that met their and our highest expectations. Our job was to use our imagination to define those expectations.

Glad to be Here: Elise

At a monthly breakfast, Elise and I happened to sit together.

"Well, I'm glad I'm here and don't have to worry about a lot of things," said Elise, who paused a moment. "What's really bothering me, though, is the thought that I may get Alzheimer's. That'd be terrible."

I made no comment, just listened, and she continued:

"I'm the youngest of six. Our mother had Alzheimer's, three of my siblings had it, and three of them had diabetes as well. So far, I'm okay, and I'm grateful for that. When you have those kinds of things on your mind, it's easy to overlook little annoyances and focus on the positive."

"Yes," I said. "Cancer survivors say the same thing. When you've walked the narrow path of facing your own death, you learn to appreciate the good and mostly ignore the bad."

She reminisced: "I came from a very poor background. When I was seven, my father left us. He said he was going to sell the car to get us a little money, and he drove off. He never returned. We had no reason to suspect foul play. He just didn't come home. Sometime later – weeks or months, I'm not sure – he sent a letter. Something about a man who picked him up and took his money and dropped him off somewhere else. So, we knew he was alive, but then we never heard from him again."

I asked, "Did he have problems that you knew about – Alcohol? Health? Anything like that?"

When she shook her head "no," I speculated. "He must have been terribly burdened by the impossible responsibility of having a wife and six children and no money for them. ... It's sad that he saw escape as his only way to manage. What awful demons must have followed him. And you never knew what happened. Maybe he ended up with a new family. Or not."

I continued, "What did your mother do? She had six children to raise."

"Well, the oldest was seventeen. He had already left. He and our dad didn't get along, so he'd already gone to Chicago to live with our uncle. He returned for a while after Dad left, but then he went back.

"Another brother, who was about fifteen at the time, 'borrowed' a car. When the police caught him, they gave him a choice: jail or military, so he joined the Army.

"My mother did work wherever she could find it. She took in laundry. She cleaned houses. We stayed together. I'm grateful for that and for all the hard work she did. She never graduated from high school, but she made sure I could, and I did. Then I went to Bible College. I was able to take the trolley-line each day.

"And you know what? My mother started taking classes there too. She wasn't working on a degree or anything, she was just interested in the Bible and curious about what she could learn from the teachers there.

"So, I started out poor. I've never complained, and I've always appreciated every good thing that happened to me. I had a good life, a good husband and family, and now I'm glad for being here."

136

9: Getting to Yes

What counts in feeling happy is the group of people you live among. If you choose your community with care, then regardless of which apartment or cottage you select, you are ready to be happy, safe, and healthy.

> **And now let us welcome the new year,**
> **full of things that have never been.**
>
> **— Rainer Maria Rilka**

When what to my wandering eye
should appear but ten extra
pounds on hips, thighs, and rear.

Interlude 2: Stories of Heritage

Beyond paperwork and visits, your search for a retirement community uncovers some of the interesting residents you may live among. Relaxing in conversations with others, you share stories big and little about yourself and your family. People like to reflect on their roots. Sometimes they reminisce by telling stories about their forebearers.

Fascination: Damien

Writing in careful cursive, Damien described his collection of museum miniatures: "I come from an all-German background going back some nine generations. Between ages ten and fourteen, I spent much time after school at the Museum of Archeology at the University of Pennsylvania in Philadelphia.

My collection of Egypt-themed pieces began with the acquisition of a twelve-inch-high Nefertiti and has continued for fifty-six years. I've been to Egypt and cruised the Nile, explored the insides of the Pyramid of Khufu, Deir el Bahri (Hatshepsut), Abu Simbel (Ramses II), Temples at Karnak and Luxor, The Valley of the Kings including the tomb of Tutankhamun, etc. Why do I love it? I live in the Past!"

Christmas: Stella

In 1970, my family of three was living in a tiny apartment in married student housing at Purdue University. Full of optimism for the future, we nevertheless were hundreds of miles from home, with money only for necessities. Store-bought holiday trimmings were out of the question, but we still wanted to celebrate.

From a huge cardboard box we'd salvaged, we cut three four-foot-high silhouettes of a Christmas tree. We notched and fitted them together to make a stand-up tree, then painted it green. We trimmed it with paper snowflakes and strings of popcorn and cranberries.

Centered on the window sill of our small living/dining/kitchen room, the tree looked festive. What made Christmas Day special, however, was Mother Nature. For only the second time in my life, even until now, snowflakes fell gently all Christmas morning.

Looking beyond our quirky tree at the wintry scene outside, we were in a swirling snow globe full of peace and plenty.

Perseverance: Alfred

Born in 1906 on the Eastern Shore of Maryland on a farm touching the Choptank River, Portia's dad, Alfred, wanted something from life other than farming. He headed for Detroit, whose young auto industry was an employment hub. He journeyed by train, remembering his Aunt Grace's advice when at eighteen he visited her in Manhattan: stand tall, look confident, keep your suitcase in your hand or on the floor between your legs, be wary. This lesson in caution was life-long: in his early years, no more than five dollars ever showed in his wallet, the balance hidden beneath a flap. His friends assumed he was always broke.

In the beginning, struggling to find a steady job, Al boarded at several homes. Finding and keeping a roommate was hard – he said a fellow either lost his job and went back home or got Cupid's bite and married. Ambitious, Alfred enrolled in a Business English class at night-school. He scrambled; he paid attention.

In 1928, his Aunt Grace counseled, "Much depends on what kind of people you get in with, how your future shapes itself. Keep in with successful people and avoid people with a grudge against the world generally. They are either failures or have indigestion and should see a doctor. ... Stick it out, Alfred, and get yourself ready to fit into a definite and useful place in the world. For after all, there is no use living, unless you make the world better because you have lived."

Through the Depression, he persevered. He needed to pay for a hernia operation for which, he wrote his mother, "the doctor's bill was $100, the hospital bill $69, and assorted sundries bringing the total to $200, leaving the bank account with only $40."

By age thirty, Alfred's circumstances were improving. "Yesterday I went to the airport and took a ride with the fellow who gave me my air-club membership. We flew with the dual controls in so I could show him a few stunts, loops, and rollovers. It was a thrill to have something else to think about besides personal troubles. If I could only fall heir to a plane and money to fly it, I could sail right through this Depression, whoopee!"

He advanced into responsible positions first as manager of a Kroger store and then into the rapidly growing tractor-trailer industry. Finally, his big break came when he worked at the Detroit office of the Fruehauf Trailer Company. A few years later, after moving the family to Philadelphia, he rose to Service Manager; later, he became a seasoned salesman and then a junior executive in the Manhattan office. Although he never bought a plane, he flew small craft on weekends and in retirement participated in the Civil Air Patrol.

Lifelong, he peered at every tractor-trailer sharing the highway and gazed aloft at every flying craft, be it plane, helicopter, hot-air balloon, or ultra-light. With modest demeanor and quiet leadership, he modeled a standard of sterling achievement: do what you love, love what you do.

Migration: Beverly

My father was Russian, but German. His parents were German, but he had been born in Russia. A few years earlier, with two or three small children, they had emigrated from Germany to the Ukraine, which was then a part of Russia.

Catherine The Great had sent advertisements all over Europe seeking immigrants to settle in Ukraine. She lured poor people with promises of abundant land and comfortable housing. My grandparents must have been struggling in Germany. They were probably just a few generations from peasants living feudal lives. Healthy and eager, they welcomed this chance for a better life for their young family.

They bought passage on boats that took them to a port in northern Russia, then by river past Leningrad and Moscow and further south by train into remote Ukraine. At the last station, they boarded a wagon pulled by oxen, for a sixty-mile trek to the middle of nowhere. The roads must have been only ragged trails.

What a disappointment. No farms, no housing, no town, no assistance. At first, they had to live in a cave. The Empress's promises of prosperity had turned into a shell of subsistence living. They yearned for the privations of their former German lives where at least they could speak the language and have friends and family nearby.

I'm not sure how they heard about emigrating from the Ukraine in Russia to America, but that's what they did. With a pittance and their promises to work off their debt, they packed up their now-larger family, including my two-year-old father, and made their way back to the ocean port to sail across the great Atlantic Ocean. Their transport ship crossed in ice-filled shipping lanes just two days before the Titanic met its iceberg on April 15, 1915. Imagine!

My father's story makes me think. No one wants to pack a few essential items, abandon the rest, and leave home. No one wants to say goodbye, probably forever, to family, friends, mother-tongue, everything that's familiar. Only a miserable or frightening life could force that kind of decision.

I'm a child of an immigrant. So is everyone I know. That's what America is. This world-wide issue of immigration takes on an entirely new meaning when I let myself empathize with the refugees I see on TV.

Pioneer: Lib

Mary Elizabeth (Lib), Polly's great-grandmother, was born in 1860 in Ontario, Canada, and died at eighty-seven years old. Petite but mighty, she left a legacy of letters that reveal her inner grit:

We were forty-three days in a covered wagon on the journey from Topeka to what used to be called Indian Territory. Six weeks and one day through rain and shine, heat and cold. Finally, we pulled up at the boundary line that separated the United States and Canada. It looked like all the other prairie we had passed through. I turned to Will and said, 'All that driving, Pa, for this?'

but my husband said, 'A woman is no judge of land. Why Lib, this is the best land that lies outdoors.'

We arrived on the seventh of June 1883, and this land became our home for eighteen long years. Another woman might have complained, 'So many miles through creeks and over hills, to land in an out of the way place like this and have to call it home.' As for me, I was just thankful to get my feet on the ground and stay there.

It was about three in the afternoon. Will and I and our little girl were all hungry. We drove over the boundary line into Canada to a tiny house that Herbert had rented for us.[26] Horses and wagon rattled to a stop, and we climbed out. Herb was making a fire to get supper. Was he surprised! 'Well, Lib,' he said, 'I will let you get supper.'

I'd been fixing Will only this 'n that for two or three days now, so I wanted him to have a good meal the first night we reached home. I hurried around and cooked our supper on a real stove. For six weeks and a day, I had cooked using three long irons instead of a stove. Each evening Will had pounded two forked iron rods into the ground, and onto them he placed a cross-iron where I hung my kettles. On this magnificent arrival day, I cooked indoors. Truly, we were home.

The next day we all drove back to North Dakota to our land that Uncle Sam had promised us. A more beautiful country I have never seen than was spread out before us. A clear little creek called the Cypress lay at our feet, edged here and there with deep, water-filled gulches called coulees and pretty little groves

---

[26] Herb and Bob were Will's two brothers who, along with Lib's brother Sid, had preceded them.

of wild cherry trees. Will chose this spot for our family. The constant flow of fresh water would provide good grazing pasture for the cattle. Nearby another grove of wild choke cherry trees and willows lay right at the foot of the hill below. It was beside one of the little coulees that we would soon build our home.

We pitched our tent on our claim. My brother Sid had already made his choice, and Will's brothers Bob and Herb picked their claims. The week after we arrived, Will, Bob, and Herb took the three teams and went to Neche, a town in North Dakota about fifty-five miles due east from us. It had been settled two years earlier and had stores and supplies. Their little group would have to haul the lumber back over two mountains, taking a week altogether.

When the brothers returned with the lumber, a Canadian neighbor helped us, along with Bob and Herb, both bachelors. Within a week, the men built Nellie and me a home twenty-feet square. I was as proud as any woman of today in her modern bungalow. Our claims being immediately south of the border, ours was the last farm north in the United States. I was the first woman settler in Cypress Township, and Nellie the first child. I was twenty-three years old. ...

"One day when Will was threshing in Canada, I had bread baking and was patching the clothes. Without a knock, the door opened and an Indian boy about eighteen stepped into my small abode. I was so frightened I could hardly speak. He knew he had frightened me. He stepped over to the stove and commenced rubbing his hands. He said, 'Pretty cold.' I was too frightened to sew or speak. I knew that an Indian uprising just twenty years earlier had driven out most settlers except those in the Pembina country where we were.

The needle quivered in my fingertips. I thought if I opened the oven door to check my bread, I would get over my scare. The loaves were golden-crusted, and I commenced removing them to the table-top. The young Indian asked, 'How much you want for one?' I replied, 'Ten cents.' I had five loaves, and he said, 'I take all,' and handed me fifty cents. Without another word, he lifted each loaf into a sack and left as quietly as he came.

I locked the door and collapsed into a chair. Only then did I count the coins at the edge of the table. They were the first money I had of my very own since we'd left sunny Kansas."

"Mud on My Face?" Edith

Lib's second daughter Edith (Polly's grandmother) had her own stories to tell. Here's how she met her future husband:

Nellie Hazlitt Bassingthwaighte and her eighteen-year-old sister Edith Hazlitt were having lunch with a favorite cousin Harry Hazlitt in Sarles, North Dakota, one pretty summer day in 1908. Dressed in their finest clothes, the two young ladies had driven to town in the Bassingthwaighte buggy drawn by Nelly's husband Joe's very spirited racehorse, Jim.

After lunch, Harry returned to work, and Nelly and Edith started for home. Before they had gone far, it began to rain, and the girls reached for the umbrella. One of them raised it rapidly, and Jim, wearing no blinders, became frightened at this quick action and bolted.

Both girls hung onto the reins, screaming 'Whoa Jim – whoa Jim,' which only added to the poor beast's fright, and on he went with a fresh burst of speed. The harness suddenly gave way, and the two girls flew out of the buggy as it flipped over on its side, plopping them into fresh mud. After picking themselves up and ascertaining that they were not injured, Nellie volunteered to walk back to town and enlist Harry's aid. Edith was to wait near the buggy.

Before long, a dapper young man came driving by. Sizing up the situation, he offered to drive Edith into town or perhaps meet Harry and Nellie on their way back. Edith gratefully climbed in, and as they rode along, she appraised the young man beside her and decided, 'hmm, not bad!'

Then, aware of her disheveled appearance, she smoothed her hair, tried to brush the dust and mud from her dress, and innocently inquired, 'Do I have any mud on my face?'

That was too much for the young man, and after giving her an amused look, he replied, 'I should say you have!' and burst out laughing. The young man turned out to be Ole Pladsen, a neighboring farmer. Before long, Edith and Ole were dating – and to borrow a phrase – 'You know the rest.'

Many times over the coming years, their children heard Ole say, 'I should say you have,' words that always brought a smile to his lips.

Sick Baby: Louise

Edith and Ole's eldest daughter Louise, also liked writing family stories such as this one:

Mother and Dad had seven children. When the fifth one, Phyllis, was a baby about ten months old, Mother was nursing her with an ample supply of breast milk. However, one of our neighbors, Mrs. Mitchell, was in deep trouble with her tiny baby boy. He had mouth sores and was wasting away with little hope of survival. Prepared baby formulas didn't exist in those days. It was a choice between cow's milk or mother's milk, and this little fellow's mother had no milk. The doctor told her that the baby would surely die soon without getting mother's milk.

Here we were, with me eight years old, Paul, Marge, Doris, baby Phyllis and our Dad, living in a small house with no conveniences at all, and Mother trying to decide if she could nurse the sick baby as well as Phyllis too.

In such dire circumstances, she could not refuse. So, every four hours, here came Mrs. Mitchell with her baby and little 'Noonie,' her four-year-old son. Mother would get such a strained look on her face when she saw them coming. She would nurse Phyllis first, then wash her nipples carefully, then take the tiny babe and nurse him. The mother would sit nearby, and Noonie cavorted around.

That was one of the worst tasks I ever saw Mother go through. The sad part was that after some time, the babe died anyway. He was just too weak to suck out enough milk to help him grow.

The next Christmas, a big carton arrived from the Mitchells. In it was a cut-glass bowl called a 'fern dish' with a silver inset, and a beautiful cut-glass cream and sugar set, in appreciation of what Mother had done.[27]

---

[27] Recollections from three generations of strong women who liked to write letters: **Elizabeth** (1860-1947); her daughter **Edith** (1890-1978); her daughter **Louise** (1910-1994), as related by Louise's daughter in the fourth generation who herself has a daughter and a granddaughter.

10: Downsizing

Questions: When should I begin downsizing? What is a downsizing plan that works? How can I make the hardest decisions about letting go of things I treasure? What shall I keep, and where can I take, give, sell, and discard the things I part with? How can downsizing be life-expanding?

There are many avenues to success in downsizing. You can do a lot or a little. You can get it done in two years, as Don and I did, or in a month, as some of my Rolling Meadow neighbors did. You can organize your tasks and work methodically or tackle them in a free-form fashion that suits your time and personality.

Some people move nearly everything they own and find ways to live with it all or to deal with it later. Others want the job done now so they can enjoy pursuing other activities in their new home.

There is no "right way" that will work for everyone. In fact, your way will likely be your own personal combination, for you are tailoring your future based on the lifestyle you've established over the years. As for me, I enjoyed the sense of accomplishment that I gained as I learned how to let things go. I felt liberated.

Email from a friend: Good luck with downsizing – it's real work and not a whole lot of fun, but it will feel amazingly satisfying. Advice: when in doubt, throw it out! (Really, give it away if you

can.) Your new place will feel more quickly like home if it is not overstuffed. My best, Joan.

Make a Plan

If you decide to move to an LPC or anywhere else, you can find a way to downsize. As I describe the system that worked for Don and me, you will adopt some ideas, reject others, and create still others. You'll develop the plan that works for you. If you give yourself plenty of time, you can enjoy your progress and love the results.

Two years before moving to Rolling Meadow, I began downsizing. I remembered a friend in New Jersey who had bought her retirement home in Idaho three years before driving across the country to settle into it. Every week, she filled a big trash-bin with two or three bags of discards, a manageable task in her busy life. I too set a long-range goal: I would downsize *something* every week. Husband Don, politely disinterested, felt that "several years from now" was too distant to envision. For me, though, long-range planning is fun.

Downsizing became my hobby.

First, I decluttered. Pretending a realtor's Open House was imminent, I removed all items lying casually around the house such as pencils and pads, coasters, magazines, tissue boxes. I boxed up table-top and windowsill items such as souvenirs and small photos. Then I removed half the wall art, remembering a realtor's advice that a house has more character when the seller leaves a few paintings on the wall. These actions, done over two weeks, made our home look cleaner, neater, brighter, and bigger. Surprise: our streamlined house was easier to keep orderly. My feelings ballooned: I can do this!

Yes, there is joy in making a home look its best and stay that way. In her handbook *the life-changing magic of tidying up*, Japanese author Marie Kondo undergirds her practical tips with elements of Shinto philosophy: she explains how inner joy comes when we respect the spirit within each object we love.

> **... the best criterion for choosing what to keep and what to discard is whether keeping it will make you happy, whether it will bring you joy. ... Keep only those things that speak to your heart. Then take the plunge and discard all the rest. By doing this, you can reset your life and embark on a new lifestyle.**[28]

Early in her book, Kondo summarizes her advice: she says you should always think in terms of category, not place.[29] For example, I learned to say, "next I'll work with cookware" (not "I'll go to the kitchen"); "I'll work with paperbacks" (not "I'll sort the books"); "writing tools" (not "clean out the desk"). The more I subdivided household contents into specific categories, the more efficiently I could work. By the way, I discovered that, once I realized that I had multiples of the same things, such as spiral notebooks, I saved money because I did not buy more.

Clothes, Papers, Books, Magazines

First, I tackled **CLOTHES**.

I had never thought about categories of clothing. Writing to a friend, I reported:

> **Organized! I spent parts of four days implementing Marie Kondo's plan for sorting, selecting, and storing my clothes. My first category was "tops": short sleeve, long sleeve, turtleneck, knit, cotton, winter, summer. I made up my own criteria: Does it**

---

[28] Kondo, Marie. *the life-changing magic of tidying up: the Japanese art of decluttering and organizing.* Ten Speed Press, 2014, 42.
[29] Kondo, 43.

fit? Is it my color? Does it make me feel confident? If three answers were 'yes,' I kept it; if any answer was 'no,' I folded it for the discard box. The keepers I folded or hung according to Kondo's suggestions.

Sorting tops took nearly three hours, and I stopped for the day. On subsequent days I did the same process with other categories of clothes: pants, dresses, skirts, sweaters, coats, shoes, underwear, and accessories (belts, hats, purses). Each day, for two to three hours, I took care to start and finish just one category. By assuring that my energy equaled my ambition, I enjoyed the work.

Now, for the first time since college, ALL my clothes are neatly arranged in either my four-foot-wide closet or my bureau of six drawers, and all my shoes are arranged on a three-foot wide, two-tier shelf on the closet floor. No longer will I have to switch wardrobes at the seasons; all my clothes are in plain sight and color-coded; everything is easy to select and easy to put away. I invested ten hours and already reap rewards.

Subdividing 'clothes' into six or seven morning projects worked great: I kept my enthusiasm, the bedroom was orderly at the end of each session, and immediately I was rewarded for my effort. Also, I learned I can do a daunting downsizing task because I understood Marie Kondo's process and followed her directions.

Next on the list is organizing the category of 'paper.' Later, 'kitchenware' and then 'photographs.' I agree with the book title, for already Marie's approach is life changing.

In files, drawers, and boxes, I had **PAPERS** galore: medical and tax files, copies of reports, stacks of students' exams from years ago, letters, greeting cards, a postcard collection, cancelled checks, household bills, insurance papers. You know!

From Marie:

I recommend you dispose of anything that does not fall into one of three categories: currently in use, needed for a limited period of time, or must be kept indefinitely. ...Do not sub-file papers, especially ones that you have to keep indefinitely. Just keep them all in one file-folder.[30]

Burrowing into files and boxes, shredding a LOT of old medical and financial files, I reminded myself that these records are available online. Some boxes had files so old they puffed dust when I handled them. Many carefully organized files I could simply dump, for their neat labels were dated long ago.

BOOKS came next, shelves of them throughout the house: technical, historical, fiction, old, new, unread, to be reread, large, small, hardback, paperback, plus stacks of **MAGAZINES**. Setting my own criteria now, I made invaluable guidelines: "Will I ever read (or re-read) it? Why did I keep it? Why might I ever want it?" After just an hour that first day, four boxes of donations went into the car, and in subsequent days I added nine more, all to donate to the library's used-book sales and to the local thrift shop. Other volumes and most magazines went into the trash. I removed a few bookshelves and combined others so that our books and magazines were clustered in just two areas, orderly and appealing.

From a friend: When Gary and I downsized to a house half the square footage, it was one of the most liberating experiences of my life. There were boxes in the basement, I didn't even know

---

[30] Kondo, 97.

what was in them, not to mention the attic. We threw them out unopened. We had a rule: If we hadn't used it in the last month, we tossed it, except of course Christmas decorations. We rented a dumpster and filled that puppy to the brim. Our new rule is if something new comes into the house, something old must go. I cannot tell you how much easier life is.

Working with clothes, papers, and books had taught me the **rules**:

1. From every room, gather everything that's in its category.
2. Divide the task into small parts.
3. Work in units of two to four hours.

I realized important **corollaries**:

1. When energy starts to falter, stop for the day: I don't have to finish the category in one go.
2. Sometimes it's wise to do a once-over now and an in-depth later, after my mind has had time to reflect about those items.
3. Some categories take days; some, weeks; a few require months.

In a nutshell, my motto is "Work when it's fun, I'll know when I'm done."

Kitchen

Downsizing the **KITCHEN** required multiple blocks of time. After all, think of the categories: cookware, bakeware, flatware, utensils, dishes, serving pieces, glassware, aprons/dish towels/oven mitts/hand towels, cookbooks/recipes, counter-top appliances. A kitchen is overwhelming until you divide it into categories.

For example, I discovered that I had abundant duplicates: four sets of measuring spoons and three sets of measuring cups; eight long carving/slicing knives; fifteen commemorative coffee mugs. I had unused barbeque skewers, pie-crust weights, individual covered butterdishes. Pretending I was at a flea market, I could choose, for *free,* the nicest one of everything and then give away all the others or take them to the thrift-shop.

Working two or three days a week for nearly a month, I saw my kitchen transform from decades of "stuff" to an organized workplace containing only what I used. During the process, I was also assessing my attitudes toward cooking and eating, to wit: I no longer entertain, I do not enjoy cooking, I prefer light meals and few desserts. Thus, I had pleasure in saying farewell to things like large pots, electric mixer, and most bakeware and serving pieces. Further, I discovered how much I looked forward to living in a retirement community that has a tasty Dining Room!

Although we can get to know ourselves better by sitting down and analyzing our characteristics or by listening to others' perspectives on us, I believe that tidying is the best way [to discover who we are]. After all, our possessions very accurately relate the history of the decisions we have made in life. Tidying is a way of taking stock that shows us what we really like.[31]

That Will to Divest
Meaning: once
you've swept
the shelves
of spoons
and plates

---

[31] Kondo, 176.

> **you kept**
> **for guests,**
> **it gets harder**
> **not to also**
> **simplify the larder,**
> **not to dismiss**
> **rooms, not to**
> **divest yourself**
> **of all the chairs**
> **but one, not**
> **to test what**
> **singleness can bear,**
> **once you've begun.**
> **— Kay Ryan,** *The New Yorker*, **April 12, 2010**

Photos, Sentimental Items

I had saved two categories 'til the end: **PHOTOGRAPHS** and **SENTIMENTAL ITEMS**. For a year of downsizing, I had dreaded tackling these items so infused with feelings. Then I realized I could employ the downsizing tools I'd been practicing: to make categories and to make criteria. Only I alone could make decisions about these highly personal treasures.

For example, on many mornings, I woke up thinking about how to subdivide the huge number of photos I had accumulated over a lifetime and, later, how to evaluate the antiques and mementos that filled the china cabinet. A big help was to remind myself that *the best things in life aren't things.*

For a third time, I read Marie Kondo's suggestions for **PHOTOS**:

There is only one way to sort photos, and you should keep in mind that it takes a little time. The correct method is to

remove all your photos from their albums and look at them one by one. .... When you do this, you will be surprised at how clearly you can tell the difference between those that touch your heart and those that don't. As always, keep only the ones that inspire joy. .... Really important things are not that great in number. ... we shouldn't still be sorting photos when we reach old age. ... Do it now. When you are old, you will enjoy the photos far more if they are already in a [new] album than if you have to move and sort through a heavy boxful of them.[32]

Over the years, I had made fourteen photo albums. First, I scanned their pages to the computer; then I stripped out the photos in eleven of them, saving only three albums for my permanent collection.

Upon the dining room table at its full eight-foot length, I sorted photos into nine large grocery bags each labeled with names: my name or the name of the relative who might want them, plus not one but two DISCARD bags. Bags full of photos are *heavy*.

Because pictures featuring mostly me became three bags full, I interrupted the project for three weeks to make an album called "Me" – my life within two covers. It's scanned now, and I'm keeping it, too. Every page makes me happy. Why? Because whenever a photo was unflattering or reminded me of an unhappy moment, I threw it out!

Taming all my photos took eight weeks. That's a long time, but oh, so worth it: instead of twelve or thirteen big bags of photos and fourteen albums, all I moved to our apartment were three albums and a handful of prints.

---

[32] Kondo, 118-120.

As with photos, for **SENTIMENTAL ITEMS** I also reread Marie's advice:

> ... these are the hardest things to discard. ... [but] truly precious memories will never vanish even if you discard the objects associated with them. We live in the present. No matter how wonderful things used to be, we cannot live in the past. The joy and excitement we feel here and now are more important. So ... the way to decide what to keep is to pick up each item and ask ourselves, "Does this spark joy?"[33]

Nearly all my personal treasures were behind the curved glass in the huge antique cabinet that had been my mother's pride and joy. Holding in my hand each beloved object, I took my time to say in words, "Does this object make me happy? Does it trigger a pleasant memory? Does it please me in some other way?"

Often, there was a deeper element to evaluate. Because many pieces had come from my mother, they brimmed with emotional attachment. I counseled myself: "Mother was practical, she would understand, she would love knowing what good care I've given her favorite pieces for all these years. She would not be happy that this object means less to me than it did to her, but she'd understand. She'd be glad that it will go to a new owner who will enjoy and appreciate it."

Oh, how I talked to myself, for I knew I was the only one who could persuade myself to make these hard choices.

> People never retrieve the boxes they [label for later]. ... they will never again be opened. .... By handling each sentimental item and deciding what to discard, you process your past. If you

---

[33] Kondo, 114-118.

just stow these things away ..., before you realize it, your past will become a weight that holds you back and keeps you from living in the here and now. To put your things in order means to put your past in order too. It's like resetting your life and settling your accounts so that you can take the next step forward.[34]

In my mind I was constantly sorting these sentimental items, deciding, evaluating. As days went by, I gained confidence. Choosing what to keep became easier. I took care to ensure I'd have no regrets.

Hobo's Table: Renee

When I was a little girl, my family was dirt-poor, but we got along fine. Our house was very close to the railroad tracks, maybe just fifty feet. The word got out among the hobos that my mother would give them food if they came to the back door and asked. My father made a green bench next to the door on the back porch for them. When a hobo came and asked for something to eat, she'd make him a sandwich and then say, you can have this, but you must eat it on that bench.

One day, a hobo appeared with a stick-table – a three-legged little table that you'd put a plant on. He asked my mother whether she'd care to buy it. She asked, how much is it? He said, twenty-five cents. Well, she said, I don't have an extra twenty-five cents. He said, would you give me something to eat for it? She agreed. She prepared two

---

[34] Kondo, 114-118.

sandwiches for him, and he gave her the table. On its underside, she wrote the year: 1935.

After my mother died, I brought that little table to my home. My husband said, "What do you want that old thing for?" I told him its story, and by the end, he had tears in his eyes. Here in my small apartment, that stick-table has its place. I will never part with it.

One day during those challenging weeks of sorting nostalgic treasures, I photographed every sentimental object I could find. Later, using an online photo-album service, I stuffed a hundred or more pictures into an eight-by-eight-inch slender book entitled "THINGS." This little book became my permanent reminder of the myriad memories these treasures had for me. The cover shows brilliant, autumn-orange oak leaves with these words: "The trees are about to show us how lovely it is to let things go." On the flyleaf are Donald Hall's musings:

> **The Things**
> When I walk in my house I see pictures,
> bought long ago, framed and hanging
> – de Kooning, Arp, Laurencin, Henry Moore –
> that I've cherished and stared at for years,
> yet my eyes keep returning to the masters
> of the trivial: a white stone perfectly round,
> tiny lead models of baseball players, a cowbell,
> a broken great-grandmother's rocker,
> a dead dog's toy – valueless, unforgettable
> detritus that my children will throw away
> as I did my mother's souvenirs of trips
> with my dead father, Kodaks of kittens,
> and bundles of cards from her mother Kate.
> – Donald Hall, *The New Yorker*, January 4, 2010

Start to finish, *photos* took two months, and *sentimental items* one month. The work of these three months was difficult but no longer daunting. Concluding this final, hardest part of my big task was indeed joyful.

I kept a list of my **categories**. Why? Because the list represents my pleasure in seeing the house become more spacious and relaxing:

Accessories	Fabrics	Non-Perishable
Art	Family "Valuables"	Office Supplies
Books	Financial Papers	Papers
Button Collection	Food Frames	Photo Albums
China Closet	Giftwrap	Photos
Clothes	Houseplants	Purses/Bags
Craft Closet	Jewelry	Sewing Supplies
Craft Supplies	Kitchenware	Stationery
Declutter Desk	Linens	Travel Needs
Declutter Rooms	Medical Papers	Xmas/Halloween
Desk & Supplies	Music	

Getting Rid of Things

Friends asked how we disposed of the many items that had no place in our future apartment.

Surprisingly, only a few things went into the **trash**. When we couldn't imagine how anyone could possibly use this item because it was so old, worn, or shabby, we ditched it. Most of the refuse went into recycling or trash bins. Don also made a couple of trips to the scrapyard, garnering forty or fifty dollars for metal pipes and other useless metal. Just before moving, we called a modern-style **junk man** who came to carry away the last detritus from the house, basement, and garage. We had been told that he would either pay us, because he could sell it, or we would pay him, and his price would vary according to what we were discarding. All in all, we paid a fair price, and he left the place "broom clean."

I kept a promise to our **children** that, when we downsized any-thing that they might possibly want, we would offer it to them first. Nearly every week, our two local daughters looked over the long din-ing-room table covered with stuff and considered what they wanted. We photographed and inventoried other things to email our three distant children. I photographed memorabilia from my parents' fam-ilies to offer to my many cousins. Thus, items that were meaningful to the **family** stayed in, or were declined by, the family. As other re-tirees have found, Don and I discovered that our children and grand-children wanted very few items, and the ones they chose were often a surprise. For example, they might bypass Great-Grandma's dainty sugar bowl but pick up a glass souvenir from a traveling circus.

We drove many, many carloads of boxes to the Give, Shop, & Go, a **thrift shop** with a thriving business reselling household goods, clothing, books, and more. They know their market and have a huge customer base. It and most **charities** offer to pick up large items by appointment. A Google or yellow pages search yields other sources such as Salvation Army, Goodwill, and AMVETS.

Don sold things on **eBay**. I advocated posting items only at fifty dollars or more and easy to ship; otherwise, I felt, the time and trou-ble to set up the sale seems more valuable than the cash return. However, he enjoys using eBay and was happy to make a sale at any price, even just a few dollars. He garnered several hundred dollars, satisfactory to us both.

With abandon, we used Facebook's buy/sell service, **Market-place**. We listed a huge range of stuff priced from "free" to whatever we felt was reasonable yet cheap. We kept the big goal in mind: get rid of it! Because Marketplace requires the seller to give a pickup point, which for us was our home, our children were concerned about privacy and safety: strangers would be coming to the house. However, since we'd be moving in a few months, they concurred with our plan. When possible, we named the front porch as the pick-up point; if someone needed to come inside the house, we moved items near the front door. Buyers could walk into the house only for bulky pieces such as upholstered furniture, sofa bed, wide shelf units. The huge array offered "for free" included miscellany such as large glass bowls and vases; an old rototiller; a stack of plastic desk-top files. Keeping a detailed list of every transaction, I noticed that we got more than we expected for some items, less than we wanted for others. Overall, we realized several thousand dollars, much to our astonishment, in exchange for things sold at our convenience and with no service charge.

I signed up for a firehouse **flea market** but with poor results. Like having a **yard-sale**, pricing and displaying items were a lot of work for a disappointing return. A dialog of texts illuminates my daughter's and my attitude about yard-sales:

> **Portia: Years ago, after our last yard sale, I decided they're not worth the effort.**

> **Me: Finding new owners is hard when you want to get rid of a nice or expensive item. But "nice" is in the eyes of the beholder, and anyway, hopefully, we'll feel we've already gotten its value.**

> **Portia: Yes, I agree. I concluded that it's good for me to enjoy my things, but I shouldn't think of them as having much value beyond me. When I no longer get as much value from it, I move it along. I do see a temporal element to the decision. I save some things for the future – handy to have – or for the kids in their futures – and that value of course changes as time goes by.**

Me: I said to Don that, when we're finally settled in our apartment with fewer things, I expect that my life will be simpler, easier, and therefore freer to do what I enjoy. Indeed, of all the stuff I'll still be taking, I'm pretty sure that I could cut it in half and be perfectly happy. Once we move, I want to move forward, not look back.

Where else did we send our stuff? I enjoyed offering certain things to specific people:

Email: I had fun today. To the four children across the street, grades K-3, I gave my electronic portable keyboard – it's more than a toy, sort of a first step toward a piano. Their mom emailed that the children were surprised and happy.

At 4:00 the two oldest children, both girls, grades one and three of the South Sudanese family around the corner came over. I showed them how to use the electric mixer, and we made cupcakes. When Don and I walked them home, we took not just eighteen cupcakes but the mixer, some cookbooks, recipe cards, an oven mitt, and a new tea towel. I'd previously asked their mom whether a mixer would be welcome, and she'd said, "Oh yes, Amira loves to cook and wants to be a baker when she grows up."

I love this aspect of downsizing, to just give things to people who can use them.

Here's a cherished example of finding **a new home** for a family treasure: I had hired an expert craftswoman to repair two of my grandmother's hooked rugs that she had made on the farm using fabric scraps that she had saved to make something useful. The pieces, about a hundred years old, were vibrant. I remembered Grandma as old, bent, white-haired, trembling with hand-palsy; her rugs let me see a young, straight, strong, capable wife of an orchard-

164

man and mother of eight children. I loved displaying her handwork. But knowing the throw-rugs could not have a place in our apartment, I reached out to my cousins who might also remember our grandmother from summer visits to the farm:

Email from SaraAnn: Grandma Tryphena's beautiful rug just arrived, and I am so impressed by her artistic skills. I plan to have the rug mounted so it will hang on the wall. I don't want anyone walking on it or spilling something on it. I remember my dad commenting years ago that his mother hooked some rugs that she gave to him and he used them either in college or when he and my mother were first married. But the rugs got worn out and I assume they were thrown out. He was so sorry that he hadn't taken care of them and that he no longer owned any of her handiwork. So now, whenever I look at the rug hanging on the wall, I'll think of him and his talented mother.

Lessons Learned

Overall, I discovered many things during my downsizing:

- o Break a task into categories that can be done in half-day blocks of time.
- o Gather everything in that category from all around the house into one spot, then sort them. Forever after, keep like things together.
- o Expect to process some categories more than once – and each iteration gets easier. For example, with an

abundance of kitchenware, desk supplies, art supplies, each revisit helps discover that fewer items are necessary.

o It's wonderful to have all clothes accessible all the time.
o Quit working as soon as the task becomes stressful: put it away for another day.
o Finding good homes for things is satisfying.
o I haven't missed a thing.
o The simpler my dwelling, the happier I am. I feel free.

Teamwork

Finally, don't worry about the spouse. He'll downsize his stuff in his own time and in his own way. Don told me, "I have a plan," and he did. He had been watching, learning, and forming his direction. He would declutter when the time was right. When was the right time? For him, it was when we signed the contract for our apartment, three months before the move.

Every week, Don loaded our recycling and the trash bins to the top. Clipboard in hand, he listed what needed to be done in the house and embarked on painting, repairing, trimming. He went through his clothes, shoes, books, tools, and everything else in his sphere. We were quite a team, using muscles and brains together to sort, sell, donate, discard, and box 'n label. Our work styles are different – I'm the tortoise, he's the hare – but our results were amazing, and completed on time.

Together we spent nearly two years preparing to move, but, if required to do it in a hundred days instead of a hundred weeks, we'd have done what friends Hilda and Sammy did, simply hired a dumpster and filled it, twice!

Throughout the process and even now, I admire the words of Marie Kondo:

It is not our memories but the person we have become because of those past experiences that we should treasure. This is the lesson that keepsakes teach us when we sort them. The space in which we live should be for the person we are becoming now, not for the person we were in the past.[35]

How true. Moving to a retirement community should open *new* opportunities, not rehash old memories.

One theme underlying my method of tidying is transforming the home into a sacred space, a power spot filled with pure energy. A comfortable environment, a space that feels good to be in, a place where you can relax – these are the traits that make a home a power spot.[36]

– ... when we really delve into the reasons for why we can't let something go, there are only two: an attachment to the past or a fear for the future.[37]

Aren't these statements amazing! They make me pay attention to emotional roadblocks and be poised to deal with them. Right on!

... I think the main reason tidying has this effect [of making us look and feel better] is because through this process people come to know contentment. After tidying, many clients tell me that their worldly desires have decreased; ... once they selected and kept only those things that they really loved, they felt that they had everything they needed.[38]

---

[35] Kondo, 118.
[36] Kondo, 161.
[37] Kondo, 181.
[38] Kondo, 195.

We work for years to attain expertise, respect, money, comfort. Why not strive to achieve contentment in life as well?

You won't die if your house isn't tidy, and there are many people in the world who really don't care if they can't put their house in order. Such people, however, would never pick up this book. You, on the other hand, have been led by fate to read it, and that means you probably have a strong desire to change your current situation, to reset your life, to improve your lifestyle, to gain happiness, to shine. For this very reason, I can guarantee that you will be able to put your house in order. ... pour your time and passion into what brings you the most joy, your mission in life.[39]

Remember: You are moving because you are setting yourself free to live a safe, healthy, comfortable life in a place where, among other reasons, you will preserve either the most meaningful objects or the permanent memories of what you have treasured.

After Don and I unpacked in our apartment, we were astonished to find *empty* shelves and drawers. In our robust downsizing, we had *over*prepared. We were free to be the new He, She, and We.

---

[39] Kondo, 203.

> Lives of great men all remind us
> We can make our lives sublime.
>
> Henry W. Longfellow
> (A Psalm of Life)

Be grateful that no matter how
many desserts you eat, your
earrings still fit.

11: Fitting In

Questions: How can I adjust to a smaller home? What surprises await me there? What will I do all day? How can I be active to the extent I want to be? Will I keep my friendships and activities from before? How will my new social life develop?

Email to friends: Don and I are glad we moved to Rolling Meadow. With a touch of guilt, I think of our new lifestyle as something like a resort – nice people, easy living, good food, beautiful setting, comfortable apartment. In terms of health, being here is reassuring, for if something happens, we're well situated to deal with it. Don has "a-fib," so he doesn't miss the yard-work and house maintenance, and you already know about me: Ms. Domesticity, not! We are grateful for being physically and mentally fit for what we like to do, including daily walks, reading, computer projects, and – from our former lives – plenty of bridge games and theater.

Cohabitation

Moving into a Life Plan Community is like moving anywhere: you meet new people and new customs. You want to fit in yet maintain your independence. You transition into new experiences and friend-ships.

11: Fitting In

Inside the apartment, Don and I learned how to get along together in smaller quarters. For example, as we worked side by side in half the space, our kitchen choreography developed a new mealtime pattern: He steps back from a countertop, I step in and open the drawer. Ditto the cupboards, refrigerator, sink. We laugh.

Respecting each other's independence was important. Just as in our first months of marriage, we wanted to nurture a solo/duo balance. In our case, our office and his bathroom were on one side of the living area, our bedroom, and my bathroom on the other side. When we both were in the office using a computer or the desk, we minded our own business with only occasional interruptions to share a thought or ask a question. When I wanted to focus on the big task of writing this book, we set up a card-table with laptop and other supplies in our bedroom. Since office and bedroom each had a thick door, a closed door signified, "I'm concentrating – please enter gently."[40]

To my surprise, we learned to love the stackable washer/dryer tucked into a closet adjacent to my bathroom. Its basket holds a complete California king sheet-set. Don usually washes his clothes in the afternoon; I prefer to start my laundry before breakfast. With the laundry only a few steps from wherever we may be in the apartment, keeping our clothes neat and clean is hardly a chore but a welcome distraction from whatever else we may be doing.

---

[40] Marie Kondo inspired the arrangement of my improvised 4'x4' workspace: computer, vertical file-holder, mini-hotplate holding a tall ceramic coffee-mug, a souvenir mug from Oxford University for two pens and a pencil, a white antique kitchen-match holder for lip-gloss, a crystal vase for dried flowers from a luncheon with a dear friend, and a 5"x7" photo of Don and me walking the beach hand-in-hand. The Internet radio played classical music. I never would have expected such comfort within a sixteen square foot patch of table.

In the living room, we replaced our full-size sofa with a two-seat recliner with dual controls. Whether enjoying a recorded episode of *Jeopardy* with lunch or *Masterpiece* with supper, we love our mealtimes when we eat at home.

In the glass-enclosed sunroom, we expanded the dining table to its full length to have a spacious breakfast while enjoying the views of soaring birds and ever-changing sky. Don spreads his newspapers to his right, I to my left. At that long table, in half-day mini projects, we can sort bills, arrange art and sewing supplies, do any project that suits, and then put everything away again.

On the balcony, we placed our two-seat outdoor bench next to Aunt Amy's porch rocking-chair that Don had re-webbed and painted green. In the corner is a drop-leaf acacia wood table. Every day of the year invites us to step outside for a little fresh air, and mild weather beckons us to dine, read, or do projects while enjoying birdsongs, frog croaks, and peace.

Email: I'm still figuring out this new lifestyle, learning to allocate time for many interests, activities, and people. Meanwhile, getting older means losing energy, and I regret that I cannot do all the stuff now that I easily did even five years ago. I love it here, and Don does too.

Friends

A hallmark of Rolling Meadow is its supportive ambiance. A resident quoted her grandmother who used to say,

> **There is so much bad in the best of us,**
> **And so much good in the worst of us,**
> **That it ill behooves any of us**
> **To talk about the rest of us.**

My mother said, "If you can't say something good, say nothing at all." How comfortable it is to reside in a community rooted in consideration for others.

Before moving, I had met eight or ten residents in the aquacise class at the Rolling Meadow pool. I got to know future neighbors. After the class, joining some of them in the hot-tub, I learned about upcoming trips, the monthly Ice Cream Social, and who had just had a new grandchild – or great-grandchild. A frequent refrain was, "When are you moving in? We want you here!"

The Dining Room is a wonderful place to meet people. Before they knew our names, they dubbed us "the tall ones." We had agreed that, when conversing with others, we would listen a lot and talk a little; focus on topics present and future, not past; be positive, not negative; avoid complaints, politics, and religion. We were ready.

We strove to sit with others, usually at a table for four. Someone would say, "Won't you join us?" or we'd say, "May we sit with you?" Conversation flowed freely. Good food, no hurry, no cleanup, just enjoy each person's company. Tablemates love being asked about themselves. Their eyes flash and their faces brighten as they relate favorite stories about work, family, and pastimes.

Early on, Don and I noticed that some residents say grace before their meals. They ask, would you mind if we pray, and we say, not at all, please do. We hear beautifully phrased expressions of thankfulness, each unique no matter how often the speaker may have expressed gratitude to God.

One evening, we joined two women who often eat together. They had been neighbors in their former homes before their husbands had died. While waiting for dinner to arrive, they reminisced about their home church and the parish. Billie said her

sister had been a nun and her brother, a priest. Her parents had enrolled her sister at sixth grade in a convent school and sent the son from high school straight to seminary – all this without asking them what <u>they</u> wanted to do. Well, Billie laughed, the girl left a year before taking her vows, and the boy left seminary early too.

Just then, our server brought our plates. Having deduced that Billie and Adele were Roman Catholics, Don inquired politely, would you like to pray? They were visibly startled. Yes, they said, sure, you can do that, that would be fine. Oh, said Don, we don't pray, we just thought you might want to. With that, they smiled, picked up their forks, and said, Let's eat!

Because Rolling Meadow has no required meal-plan, many residents dine at home or in restaurants. Meeting them took more time: perhaps at the monthly Ice Cream Socials, Residents' Association meetings, activities, or simply in the halls or at the coffee station. Over time, we became acquainted with many, many residents. Within a year, we learned most of their names, and most of them learned our names. There's a general understanding that "I may not remember your name, but I know who you are, and how are you today?"

Pursuits

Every retirement community offers abundant, varied, enjoyable activities that residents can accept or decline according to their interests, abilities, and desires. Some people are active all the time, some choose just a few activities, some rarely interact. Whether extrovert or introvert, high or low energy, physically fit or limited, everyone settles into the lifestyles they prefer.

The grand essentials of happiness: something to do, something to love, and something to hope for. – Allan K. Chalmers

11: Fitting In

In our hallway, Herb and Estelle own a furnished apartment but still live in their home just three miles away. In their mid-eighties, they continue to operate their own business. A son who had taken it over is himself semi-retired, but Mom and Dad continue their active leadership. Talking about their business, their eyes sparkle with enthusiasm. At our third hallway social, when twelve of us were getting to know each other better, Herb confided to Don: "Let me ask you – what do you *do* all day?" Like non-residents who suppose a retirement community offers little to interest *them*, Herb and Estelle likely scan the activities to see what they would do when they finally move here. How will they occupy themselves day after day for years to come?

When Don and I arrived, we had the same feeling, that "there's not a whole lot for us to do." I expected that, after a few weeks of settling in, we would continue leading our usual low-key, busy lives, mostly within our home. Don loves to build websites: as the volunteer webmaster for about ten not-for-profit organizations, he creates and maintains their state-of-the-art sites. I love to read, dabble in art, embroider, correspond, play bridge, and go to breakfast with friends. Several times each month, both of us enjoy live plays at local theaters. We were never bored before, and we wouldn't be here. We expected that few of the abundant activities at Rolling Meadow would lure us.

Our plan was to be cautious about joining anything. We would take our time and be selective. That is good advice for any newcomer, anywhere. And yet....

My phone call came just three weeks after our move: Essie invited me to join the Art Committee. She said it meets only every two months for just an hour. Additionally, members help each incoming artist set up her or his show, and they supervise the Open House the following afternoon. There are six shows a year, with local artists scheduled ahead for the following twelve to eighteen months.

I considered the request: The time would be minimal, I already knew and liked two members, and the focus, art, reflected my interests. I figured that, if I joined this committee, I wouldn't have to join any others. Perfect. I accepted the gracious request and was warmly welcomed.

But commitments are rarely as simple as they seem, not when you enjoy doing them.

For years, I've made temari, Japanese-inspired embroidered spheres about the size of a tennis ball. Their elaborate designs and stunning colors draw the eye, and my unique creation – abstract temari – are spheres of art. Essie suggested I display them in a hallway cabinet so others could see them.

One thing led to another. Our community has three entrances, and all three lobbies have cabinets. One was empty and the other two had featured the same displays for a long time. Meanwhile, many other residents make beautiful crafts or have diverse hobbies. An idea struck me: why not use these cabinets to showcase residents' interests?

"Rolling Meadow Collections" was born. Working with residents and staff who called or emailed to describe their collections, I mounted shows in a small, a medium, and a large cabinet located in three separate areas of the community. Featured were things like palm-sized, handmade wooden trucks; crystal wine-bottle stoppers; knitted /crocheted hats and shawls; military medals for service and valor; hand-cast resin sculptures from nature; oil painting; needlework; with more on the list. Each display featured a card identifying the collector and the story behind the collection.

Placard in a Collections cabinet: Thirty-eight years ago, I bought a paperweight from my sister's friend to support his fledgling glass business. Glass art had never interested me until we visited his studio near Washington DC and watched him work. A year later I bought another paperweight in Kansas when my husband and I visited a glass studio there. One paperweight is nice; two is a collection. We visited other glass studios and even took lessons in Corning NY to learn glass-art techniques. Over the years the collection grew.

Paperweights are surprisingly sturdy. Children have examined these paperweights, and not one has been damaged. On their return visits, children make beelines for their favorites. My collection recalls wonderful memories of trips across the country and of some of the artists who created their works of glass art.

Not only was I visiting and photographing residents in their apartments, but I was also linking the featured person with other residents and staff. Meanwhile, the project suited me: I liked interviewing, writing, and exhibiting. I invested about five hours each for about one display every four to six weeks, totaling about forty hours a year.

My plan to join one committee for one hour every two months had morphed into a popular feature of Rolling Meadow. Saying yes to one request had developed into a new creative activity that I enjoyed.

Because of the temari display, another activity opened to me. On Thursday evenings, Knutty Knitters meets from 7:00-8:00 PM. Many come early to nab preferred seats, so by 7:00 anywhere from nine to fourteen women are sitting in a circle on the sofa, easy chairs, and folding chairs in one of the common areas. At 8:00 PM, as if a mysterious mist has suddenly suffused the area, everyone says their farewells and departs. Most attendees knit, a few crochet, I do needlework, and one or two come just for conversation.

Like a sewing circle from former times, the group chats, jokes, laughs, asks questions, tells stories, all with an easy give and take. Newcomers come who have not knitted in decades. A cabinet holds a box of donated knitting and crochet needles, another cabinet has skeins of donated yarn, and mentor/student sit side by side to start a project. Most knitting is for donations to churches, children's hospitals, and women's shelters, but everyone can work on whichever project suits her.

One evening, Rosa, an expert needle worker, was completing a white, twenty-inch-round, crocheted doily for her granddaughter's wedding. "Oh my goodness," she exclaimed, "I've made a mistake. Nearly an hour's work, and I'll have to take it all out," and she began pulling the thread and wrapping it around her fingers. "That's what I do," she said calmly; "I rip, and I reap." This wasn't the first time she had ripped out mistakes while she was reaping the pleasure of everyone's company.

Rosa mentioned that she and her husband, Clark, were looking forward to the wedding, and someone asked, "How did you two meet?" Fingers busy, she smiled. "Oh, you don't know? It's a nice story," and she began:

Young Love: Rosa

It started with our parents. As a young bachelor, my father, a Canadian, was in mission service in Egypt. When he came home on leave, various young church couples invited him to visit their congregations and to have dinner, sometimes to stay overnight, in their homes.

On one of these visits, one of the guests was a young woman who seemed very attractive to my father, and he began courting her. She accompanied him to church events, and they probably took walks together too. After six months, he proposed to her, she accepted, and they were married in Canada just before the two of them returned to continue his missionary service in Egypt. The next year, I was born.

Clark's parents were one of those host couples, and Clark was just a little baby at the time.

When I was about four, my family moved back to Canada. Church business brought Clark's family and mine together occasionally. When Clark was seventeen, I don't know why, he was smitten with me. Naturally, I gave him not a thought. I was more interested in boys my own age and other parts of my teenage world. But Clark did not give up.

Whenever our paths happened to cross, Clark wanted to spend time with me, and sometimes he wrote to me. By the time I was seventeen, I decided he was alright, and we became a couple.

When I was eighteen, I got a letter telling me I had to choose which citizenship I wanted to have on my passport. I had to choose among three: Canadian because of my parents, British because Britain at that time was active in the Suez Canal region, or Egyptian because that was the country of my birth. Of course, I chose Canadian.

When I was nineteen, and Clark was twenty-three, he proposed, and I accepted. But my father said I had to wait to marry until I was twenty-one, and of course I observed my father's wishes.

After we married, we moved from Canada to the U.S. to live near Clark's work in Pennsylvania. That first year, each month on the same date as our wedding date, he gave me a rose for every month we had been married. One rose in month one, two roses in month two, and so on. On our actual anniversary, he presented me with a dozen red roses. He wanted to photograph me holding them, and oh my, I was so embarrassed to pose for that picture because I looked so big and pregnant. Our daughter was born just a few days later. Our little girl and the roses made a beautiful armful that I love to remember!

As for Don, he kept a low profile in our community longer than I did, but when the president of the Residents' Association asked him to join the Building and Grounds Committee, Don recognized a fit suitable for his eagle-eyes and analytical mind. He said "Yes." At the end of our first year, he accepted a request to become its chairman.

Nearly every day since moving here, we've walked a mile on the campus, either indoors or out. When Don sees a problem big or small, he photographs it to show what and where it is and sends a work request to Maintenance for repair or replacement. Burnt out lightbulbs? Squeaky hinges? Fire-doors failing to latch? Faucet dripping in a restroom? Wasp-nest constructed in high branches? Hornets zooming from a stump? Carpenter bees drilling into a hillside bench? The maintenance team makes repairs promptly. After all, residents, administration, and marketing all want our community to be its best. Within months of our arrival, Don found a satisfying activity using his skills in observation, organization, problem-solving, and communication – or did it find *him*?

Residents volunteer to serve in ways they like. Some fill water-pitchers for bed-bound residents in Skilled Nursing; others escort wheelchair-bound residents from Assisted Living to a presentation about ancient Egypt; others read to residents whose eyesight has failed. Volunteers prove the adage, "many hands make light work." They do tasks that might otherwise require paid help, equivalent to thousands of dollars in saved money, helping to trim our community's annual budget and thus saving *us* money. Further, they contribute to the social fabric of Rolling Meadow, a treasure that cannot be measured in dollars.

In a caring, sharing community, residents can count on supportive friends and staff in both good times and bad:

Voluntary Service: Preston

After serving nearly twenty-two years in Indonesia and sixteen years on the staff of a local church, I had the opportunity in 1999 to do something that I had always wanted to do: serve as a chaplain of a retirement community. ... I decided that since I would be working with senior adults, I should enroll in an eighteen-hour gerontology certificate program sponsored by the medical school downtown. My final course was to write a paper on seventeen ingredients in successful aging.

One of the things that I learned came from a series of studies by the National Institute of Health that concludes that senior adults living in retirement communities live longer and are happier not because people do things for them but rather, because they do things for others. Whenever I hear people say, 'I have done my share of things during my lifetime, and now I really do not want to get involved in anything,' I frankly feel sorry for them. They will miss the joy of continuing to live purposeful lives, and their worlds may well be confined to the four walls of their apartments.

I was discussing the issue of volunteers with our volunteer coordinator, Meredith Thompson. Meredith told me that last year the total number of volunteer hours known to her amounted to 10,800. If we would add the number of hours involved in committee work, the Residents' Association, and the work that we informally do each day, that number may double or even triple. At Rolling Meadow, it is hard to find people 'sitting on their hands' waiting for something to do.

As the president of the Residents' Association, I want to thank each of you who give of yourselves to help fellow residents in their times of need and who provide an atmosphere, as we partner with the administrative staff, to make Rolling Meadow the 'flagship' of retirement communities in our area. I want to strongly encourage you to continue to use your time, abilities, and energy to show how much you care for your fellow residents. I can guarantee that you will be happier knowing that you have made a difference in the lives of 'family' members here in our community.

So Much to Do, So Little Time

What else do Don and I do? Studying the monthly lists of exercise classes, lectures, study-groups, movies, games, and more, I saw more to do than time to do it. That was a surprise. I found myself saying, "I'll save *that* for when I'm old." Sometime in the future, for example, I plan to attend a Saturday night movie, play bingo, learn pinochle, enjoy a Bach at Noon concert, join the mystery book-club. Someday, I may need to sign up for shopping trips to a grocery store or Walmart or the dollar-store, or I'll join a restaurant outing for lunch. For now, I exercise at chair yoga and balance classes, attend illustrated talks about the Civil War, shop at the resident-run annual Indoor Sidewalk Sale, teach a temari class, paint in the Art 'n Craft Studio. Meanwhile, from my pre-community life, I still attend my monthly book group, weekly bridge game, and bimonthly breakfasts with friends.

What do I do all day? I'm busy!

Friendship Across the Ocean: Amelia

Thanks for inviting me to your apartment to choose a temari for my friend Setsuko in Japan. These are so pretty, and I don't know whether she has seen them in Japan, but her eighty-third birthday is in two weeks, and every year I like to send her a gift, so she'll know I'm thinking about her. She was originally my high-school friend Irene's pen-pal for over fifty years starting when Irene was thirteen and Setsuko was seventeen. I first met Setsuko in 1990 on one of her visits to Irene in Michigan. A few years later, when Irene died, I used email to let her friends in other countries know the sad news.

Setsuko wrote back, and I wrote to her, and then WE were friends. Even at seventeen, she had been studying English, and through the years she gave English conversation classes at the Y in her city of Nagoya. She loved to travel to other countries and, after Irene died, Setsuko returned at least three times to Michigan to visit my family and Irene's husband Bruce. She wanted to do just ordinary things like buy groceries and go to doctor and dentist appointments. She even went with me to my chemo infusions and a post-op visit after my knee-replacement. She has two sisters, Saduki in Osaka and Kimiko in Yokohama.

When their father was in the Japanese army in World War Two, he was captured and imprisoned in the Philippines. For five years they never heard from him and assumed he was dead. Then one afternoon a bent, emaciated man walked up their front path. They didn't recognize him, so they were stunned to discover he was their father.

Setsuko was divorced many years ago. She is a resolute person. She has several daughters but only one son, Nobu. She gave her house to Nobu, so now she lives in a three-generation dwelling: Nobu doesn't work due to mental-health issues; his wife Joko is Setsuko's caretaker/helper; and their twenty-year old daughter Chiari is there too. Chiari went to college to major in theater but has an office job while she pursues her acting.

Setsuko wanted to visit us here at Rolling Meadow, but I discouraged it – that's too long a trip at her age. I don't know Setsuko's state of health these days, and I'm not even sure she's still alive, and if she is, I don't know whether she'll let me know she got this gift. But what's important is that I chose this pretty, hand-made Japanese craft, and she'll know I was thinking of her.

Energy dwindles with age. With so many activities available, one risks feeling overwhelmed. A frustration that accompanies getting older is the need to cut back. I like this rhyming wisdom recited to me by my eighty-plus friend along our one-mile morning walk:

> I looked in the mirror and what did I see –
> a face looking back. It couldn't be me!
> I'm not nearly so old or so gray or so fat
> as the face in the mirror that I'm looking at!
> I'll tell you the truth and I'm sure you'll agree
> – mirrors are not what they once used to be.

Having Less Energy

Every few years, you, along with me, may find you need to withdraw from some things to keep up with others. In fact, this motto summarizes the situation: "Do less and enjoy more." Recalibrating our expectations is positive: like dining at a smorgasbord, everything may be tempting, but we can't have it all.

From a friend, Sophia, sharing her thoughts about her mother:

> **... my hat is off to Dr. Oliver Sacks, who chose to regard old age as 'a time of leisure and freedom, freed from the fictitious urgencies of earlier days, free to explore whatever I wish, and to bind the thoughts and feelings of a lifetime together.'[41] As I read that quote, I thought of my mom. In her nineties, she continued to teach English in her home to immigrant children and adults, as that was a priority with her; but she started to firmly decline invitations to large gatherings or lunches in restaurants.**
>
> **She shared with me that she was just more comfortable at home, reading, listening to music, and crocheting. Her new schedule worked because those who really cared about her would stop in to visit frequently. As for her musings of the thoughts and feelings of a lifetime, she collected them all in her booklet 'My Life' which is now preserved for her grandchildren.**

After a few months, Don and I had developed a blend of pursuing personal interests, outside activities, volunteer tasks, and socializing with our new friends. "What do we do around here?" We're busier than ever! Days and weeks speed by at an eye-opening pace.

Other residents create their own mixes: Some continue their outside jobs part-time and even full-time. Some mostly stay in their apartments; some socialize in the halls, at the coffee bar, conversation corners, puzzle tables, or gathering places outside in the

---

[41] Krystal, Arthur. "'Old News: Why can't we tell the truth about aging?' A Critic at Large," *The New Yorker*, November 4, 2019, 77.

Courtyard. Some have furry companions: about fifteen small dogs reside here and countless cats.

At another retirement community, the CEO said, "When you live here, you can do what you want: you can stay inside all the time, you can travel any time, you can join activities and participate as you wish. No one makes you do anything you don't want to do. This is your home, and you can make it however you want it to be."

Don and I answer our non-resident neighbor Herb this way: "We do what we like to do. We're busy all the time. We feel valued, useful, and challenged. After you and Estelle move here, we think you'll feel the same!"

Parties

Something else we did not expect was "hallway socials." Organized by residents for their neighbors, mounted in a variety of locations and styles, socials pop up throughout the year. Walking the halls one winter afternoon, I came into a gathering area set with four long, folding tables and thirty-two chairs. Carrying a clipboard, Nadine was assuring that nametags and food-labels were in place. A retired teacher and an organizer, she described what was going on:

Neighbors Get Together: Nadine

About four years ago I realized I didn't know the names of some of the people on my own floor. I organized a potluck dinner so everyone could become better acquainted. I picked a day and sent invitations to everybody. We had such a good time that we've continued, with two dinners a year. They're easy and fun.

I announce the dates early: the first Wednesday in May and in December, and I tell everyone to mark their schedules now, so

they won't miss it – sometimes the first Wednesday arrives just before you turn the calendar!

Maintenance sets up the tables and chairs using a drawing I provide; we buy disposable tablecloths, plates, flatware, and drinking cups, so our only dishes to wash are the coffee-mugs and serving utensils; one of us who knows calligraphy writes nametags for everyone. Some hallways have menu themes at their dinners, but I've always kept it simple: just bring something you like, and if you're no longer able to cook, then bring something you've bought. I figure that if we have all salads or all desserts, then so be it – we'll still have a good time. It's amazing, but every dinner has a wonderful variety of dishes.

I plan games and songs too, and if we should ever run out of things to do, we can pose questions such as, "Is anyone planning a big trip?" At the end of the meal, we clean up the area and then fold the tables and chairs. That's our way to show our Maintenance person that we appreciate him – that plus the "thank you" card we've all signed and sometimes a big bowl of wrapped candy we leave for him to help himself.

About two weeks ago, a new couple moved here, but the wife was in such poor health that he couldn't care for her any longer, so she moved to Assisted Living and he's on his own. He'll be our special newcomer, and this dinner will be a great opportunity to welcome him to our hallway.

The day after Nadine described her neighborhood social, I met with Gilbert and Maud across the hall, and we planned our own hallway's first social. In our short hallway at that time, we were just twelve people, five couples and two singletons. We kept it simple: BYO beverages at four o'clock. Everyone had a great time. Then we had a pot-luck dinner, and next a pizza party. Having found success, we formalized our socials. Everyone agreed on the second Tuesday in February, June, and September at 4:30 PM. The menu varies. In our mini neighborhood, we greet a new resident with an invitation to the next hall party.

Not every party has to be planned months ahead and involve a large group. Sometimes a meet-up with a friend can be a serendipitous treat that's fun. Alma and I had met in the Wednesday yoga class where we recognized our kindred spirits. She lives a couple of miles away but has many friends here in the Meadow. By email, we planned a visit that suited just us:

Hilltop Brunch with a Friend: Stella

Let's meet at the Main Entrance and walk to the coffee station to get our coffee.

You're bringing cantaloupe? Yum!

I'll bring forks, napkins, placemats.

Here's our menu: tea-sandwiches (raisin bread, provolone cheese, tomato, cucumber, probably, w/bleu cheese dressing unless you don't like bleu cheese), a couple of biscotti, 2 chocolate truffles.

We'll walk around the campus and up the hill to the gazebo.

And if the weather turns terrible, we'll postpone it.

What a lovely morning we had, simply walking, talking, and sharing a picnic. We plucked cherry tomatoes from a patch that had grown wild from a previous year's garden, admired the beautiful solitude atop the meadow in the gazebo shading us from the hot sun, solved no world problems. Stella and I simply enjoyed each other's company.

Introspection: Anita

On the day of winter solstice shortly before the new year, Anita was evaluating her energy level:

I used to blame my low zip on the big surgery in 1991 that took over a year to recover from, but I recall junior and senior high school when, two or three times a year, I stayed home just to rest. In college and child-rearing, working, house-managing days, I'd crash on weekends with long naps. I concluded that I never had abundant energy.

Settled now into my final home, I've resolved to prioritize my low stamina: I will maintain a happy nest using the time and energy I have. I will notch down my lifestyle so that I feel happy at the end of each day.

This task sounds easy, but the problem is that, because all my activities are pleasurable, cutting back on any of them is difficult.

I listen to my feelings. Do I look forward to an activity, or dread it? I used to love attending music groups, returning home excited about what we played and what we'd tackle next. One by one, though, I dropped out of five wonderful ensembles because their energy-drain exceeded the pleasure I used to feel.

Another technique uses an imaginary balance. If I could spend a morning doing this or doing that, which one would please me more? For example, I could attend a committee meeting, write several letters, walk a mile indoors listening to a podcast, or join others at a coffee gathering. I could begin a new artwork or study a bridge convention that would improve my game.

Even six years ago, I'd have happily done all these things in a day or two. Now, I must choose.

A happy nest is more pleasing with fewer twigs.

Do less and enjoy more. That's good, and that's plenty.

Caring and Sharing: Lucille

Living in a hallway neighborhood has tender moments. Neighbors sometimes need to comfort each other in unexpected ways. Lucille noticed that the apartment across from hers was being renovated for new residents. She reminisced about its former occupants:

I liked Esther and Wayne. They were a nice couple, older but active. One night around 9:00, I helped Wayne go to bed!

It's a funny story. When I was coming back to my apartment, I saw him down the hall wearing his pajamas. I knew he had become forgetful, and I figured he was either mixed up about where he was or maybe sleepwalking.

"Can I walk you to your apartment?" I asked.

"Yes," he said, "but I'm not sure where it is."

"I'll take you there," I said, and we proceeded along to our hallway.

At the door, I knocked. Knocked again. No answer. I knew Esther was there, but she was nearly deaf.

"Maybe her hearing aids are out," I thought.

The door wasn't locked, so I entered. The apartment was dark, but there was enough light to help me guide Wayne to the bedroom where Esther was sound asleep. I got him settled on his side of the bed, tucked him in, retreated quietly, and locked the door behind me.

I used to be a nurse, so putting my neighbor to bed seemed second nature to me. The next day, nothing was said about his nighttime journey, and I never knew whether he remembered.

Mind in Decline: Murray and Frances

Murray's eyes lit up, and he responded with a smile. "What did I do? I was a minister for eight years. I went to college and majored in biology, but when I felt called, I went to seminary and was ordained. I was a parish minister for eight years. My mother-in-law was thrilled. She thought I had paved her way to heaven!

"But it turned out I didn't like my work. I grew more and more frustrated. Writing sermons was hard, and Sunday mornings came awfully fast. And I hated meetings. They happened all the time and just went on and on. I decided I had to find something else. But Frances' mother was so proud of me – she said I had paved her way to heaven."

Frances joined the conversation. "He took an aptitude test, and 'Physical Therapist' ranked high. He liked that one. At that time there were only two places in the state that offered certifications for Physical Therapy. One was four hundred miles away and the other right downtown, and that's the one that accepted him.

"We had two little boys," Frances continued. "We sold our home so the four of us could move closer to the city. We bought a house near a train station so he could commute. I found a teaching job to support us. He worked hard."

"Yes, I did," Murray said. "And you know, my mother-in-law kept on referring to me as a pastor. She said I had paved her way to heaven!"

Frances spoke up gently. "You've said that three times now, Murray. That's enough. You don't have to say it anymore."

Turning to me, she continued: "After he graduated, he worked for a hospital, and then he joined with three or four other physical therapists to make their own business. The group had hospital and nursing home contracts all over the area. They did well."

Murray went on. "It was computers that finally did me in. All the paperwork – and there was a lot of paperwork for every patient – it all had to be entered on the new computers. I hated it. And I hated losing personal touch and eye-to-eye contact. But you know, Frances's mother always liked me. During all my years as a physical therapist, she always introduced me as, 'Murray, he used to be a minister.' She was sure I had paved her way to heaven!"

Murray laughed again, happy in the moment to share a favorite memory. Frances kept her patient calmness. As for me, a newcomer, I realized that Murray may have entered early dementia. He was pleasant, outgoing, cheerful, conversational, and yet he could not remember what he had said just minutes before.

What a poignant understanding. In this community, Murray and Frances were living safe, secure lives; even so, the burden of responsibility had fallen upon Frances. I wondered how she felt about their time together both now and into the future. What has become of her inner life? What kind of personal time does she enjoy? What is her attitude towards the future?

I thought about another couple, Eric and Edith. At a general meeting, Eric mentioned that he is in an early stage of Alzheimer's. Edith continues to work part time in a local auto-repair business. Her job gives her time elsewhere with friends and

responsibilities of her own, while he is safe here with a circle of friends and activities. They both know that someday he will move to another part of the community, one with restrictions to keep him safe. He himself commented that he knows she will easily be able to visit him there even when, as he phrased it, "I might not recognize her."

Among our friends and neighbors in Independent Living are these two bittersweet examples of troubles that can happen to any of us, at any time.

Foreseeing the possibility of not just mental decline but physical ailments, some with no cure, makes one grateful to be in a place where daily life is already simple to manage, where diverse support services are handy, and where caring, abiding friendships are omnipresent.

Before moving to Rolling Meadow, I had tried to imagine what our lives here would be like. I knew we would meet nice people, live a relaxed lifestyle, and appreciate the low-key atmosphere. I had no idea, though, that we would become so involved, active, and productive. When outside friends ask, we smile and tell the truth: "The only thing we miss is the garage. Otherwise, we love it here."

12: Tales of the Pandemic

Questions: What precautions did Life Plan Communities take to keep their residents as safe as possible during Covid? What happened in Rolling Meadow during the pandemic?

> Stay home and stay safe.
> Rethink your priorities.
> It's more than just you.
> — Fran D'Angelo, International Haiku Day

The Covid response at Rolling Meadow illustrates what can happen if or when another widespread illness should appear.

In March 2020, Rolling Meadow began restrictions to reduce the likelihood of an outbreak of the deadly "novel coronavirus" that was spreading rapidly around the world. Identified in 2019, the COrona VIrus Disease was dangerous for all adults and later was deemed hazardous also to children. Covid was especially virulent for those over sixty, many of whom have fragile health or decreased immune function.

For Don and me, sheltering in place here in Rolling Meadow was not a hardship but indeed a privilege that we and most other residents appreciated. If ever the benefits of community living were apparent, this was the time.

We witnessed various responses among our neighbors.

Community: Preston

As president of the Residents' Association, Preston summarized our Rolling Meadow response to Covid:

With all face-to-face meetings on hold due to the invisible enemy, the Coronavirus, I've prepared the President's Report with this theme: "These are challenging times for us all. We're all in this together."

The words "us all" and "together" mean that we respond to the Coronavirus as a community. We all must sacrifice our individual plans and desires for the sake of the safety and well-being of every resident living at Rolling Meadow.

In Eastern culture, where Flora and I lived for sixteen years, people make decisions based on the overall benefit to the community. But in Western culture, people make decisions based on fulfilling their own purposes. We do not want anyone to tell us what to do. We do not want anyone to "clip our wings" and limit our activities. We want to do what we want to do when we want to do something.

Then, the Coronavirus comes to town, a virus that is contagious and deadly. We now need to think like Easterners who put the interests of the community over the wishes of the individual. This attitude is appropriate for us who live in a place that we call our community.

Our administration has made decisions that limit our activities in order to benefit fellow residents and staff. Let us join with hands and hearts to commit ourselves to follow our leaders' guidelines through these challenging times.

What we are asked to do and what we may not do:

1) Remain on campus until further notice. Residents who leave the campus for any reason are required to self-quarantine (stay in our apartment) for fourteen days upon our return. If there is a medical reason to leave the campus, please notify the Director first.

2) Shelter in place in our apartments. We may not congregate or walk for exercise in the hallways.

3) Wear face masks whenever we leave our apartments. Remember: my mask protects you. Your mask protects me.

4) Wash hands thoroughly for twenty seconds upon each return to our apartments.

What are residents able to do under these restrictions?

1) We may pick up our mail, waiting for someone ahead of us to get their mail before we get ours.

2) We may deliver our menu orders to the Dining Room or hand them to the person who delivers our midday meal.

3) We may get a cup of coffee at our coffee bar and return to our apartments with that coffee. The coffee bar is not a place where social interaction may take place.

4) If we receive a call that a package/delivery is in the lobby, we may pick it up or ask that it be delivered.

5) We may read newspapers in the reading room, maintaining the six-foot social distancing requirement.

6) We may walk to the trash/recycling rooms and library with the provision that we quickly return to our apartments.

7) We may walk outside around our campus, keeping social distancing in mind. We are encouraged to use the closest exit to go outside for exercise.

8) We may shop at our in-house mini mart following these guidelines: wear a mask and shop one person at a time.

9) We may use the elevators with a maximum of two people at a time to maintain the social distancing requirement.

10) If in self-quarantine, we must ask others to do our necessary errands such as dispose of our trash/recycling materials and pick up mail.

Together, we will get through this frightening time.

Working as a team comprised of residents, employees, and staff, we started the journey that seemed to have no end.

Resistance: A Letter to Annabelle

"Dear Annabelle,

"I've been concerned about you driving to the stores: You said, 'I have had such bad experiences with my orders – groceries and staples – that I prefer going myself. The car needs a ride at least once a week, otherwise the battery will die.' Annabelle, please allow the stores to deliver your items. You may not get everything you want, but you will get what you need. Let your car battery die. The battery can be brought back to life. YOU cannot.

"It's dangerous for us oldsters to expose ourselves to anyone. That other person can look fine and feel healthy but can be carrying the Covid virus without symptoms for up to four days. Giving the virus to others may be innocent, but that will be a small comfort after someone gets sick. And there is a strong possibility that we could die. In fact, I have given final instructions to my children about Wills, Medical Directives, and last wishes post-mortem. Possible death from this virus is a reality.

"Please, Annabelle, stay in your apartment ninety-nine percent of the time. Do everything you can to avoid contact with anyone else. It won't be forever."

Annabelle said thank you, but she prefers to select her own items and is sure she's safe to make short trips. Citing memories from her father's rural, home-centered doctor's office in the 1930's, she feels confident that she will be okay.

She continued to do her own thing. I reflected that she just doesn't understand. Later, however, a news column gave insights I had to consider:

Question: My mother's still going to the market and post office, even though she has an aide. …. She's 90. She knows how sick I was [with Covid], and still, there's no stopping her. I'm beside myself.

Response: … Part of the problem … is that older adults may not experience the same level of threat as younger people do. … Older adults are often masters of turning their attention away from information that is threatening, upsetting and negative.

The priority of older adults … is to make the most of their limited time on earth, and their highest value is social connection. For them, being home alone with just their thoughts and nowhere to go can be a frightening place.[42]

---

[42] Fingersh, Julie. "When Older Relatives Shrug at Coronavirus Restrictions," *New York Times*. Online, April 15, 2020.

I thought about my impatience with my dear friend Annabelle. She is eighty-nine. She gave up a career as a librarian to dedicate herself to her severely disabled son now in his sixties. With new empathy, I wrote again:

I am so sorry you are stuck in the rut called coronavirus. The whole world is in a deep pit right now, and the outlook is gloomy. It's such a terrible situation for you to be in. And others too. It's like we're all trapped in a cage and don't know when or how we can get out. Things that are important to us seem to be taken away. I'm glad you have your knitting and love of handwork, and you bake and cook for yourself and for others. The headlines say that the worst may soon be over, at least for now. Everyone will still have to be cautious. Meanwhile, scientists are working extremely hard to find answers. You and I hope that vaccines will come at the soonest possible time. As for now, we want to scream.

What else could I say?

Accommodation: Perry

Reuben and I are managing OK but really missing our old way of life. We often comment that living away from our family in rural Brazil in the Peace Corps was way easier than this social distancing of 2020. Thank goodness for FaceTime – my grandson Theo and I do chess and I'm learning to describe my moves by alpha column and numeric row – tough for grandma to master, but Hans and I are learning strategies ... yet I always seem to lose. Reuben found a low spot in the lawn to practice chipping, so he'll be ready to return to golf. We miss playing bridge with our friends. For now, we're staying safe and looking forward to the day we can do breakfast at Sammy's followed by a game of bridge.

Adaptation: Sophia

I'm fine, thanks for asking. I'm totally isolated, including not going out to any stores. I'm ordering my groceries for delivery and getting everything else online. Considering how very ill I was with bronchitis in December, I mustn't take chances. I have plenty to occupy myself here.

Yesterday my out-of-state family invited me to a FaceTime Easter dinner. They were around the dinner table with their smartphones propped up, and both grandmas were invited. That was enjoyable. For my birthday, my son's wife has offered to make any meal and cake that I choose, and Rupert will deliver it. I'm keeping in touch with my family as best we can.

We are all disappointed to miss our two grandchildren's graduations from college and high school. That is something that can never be recaptured. Also, Rupert's two children are sad because their band's tour in California this summer was cancelled, but he and I privately find a silver lining – these kids have never had to face adversity, and this will teach them that not everything in life will go as planned, and one must make the best of it.

Most of my friends do not use computers, so I have printed a "Gratitude" saying to mail with notes to each of them. I am enjoying the spring and nature more than usual – I go outside every day, even in the rain, to walk. I have always kept a bird diary so I'm noting who has just arrived (rufous towhee) and who has departed (my cute little gray juncos). Love is in the air – lots of courting going on.

Usually by now I have put away my puzzle table – a winter activity – but now plan to keep it up indefinitely. We'll keep in touch remotely until times change.

Foresight: Viola, Kathleen

Viola celebrated her Covid birthday in an unusual way:

Today this birthday girl is feeling lucky indeed for lots of reasons ... not the least of which is having friends thoughtful enough to keep in touch. At a family Zoom conference, my kids sang to me and lit a candle. Piers and I are doing an expensive take-out seafood dinner that he'll pick up at curbside late afternoon, and then we'll have dinner – with wine, of course. And we've played lots of online bridge today too. Seriously, how great a day is THIS!!??

We are bracing for a long haul because I cannot imagine Covid ending until a vaccine is available. We are poised to cancel our summer trips because, even if restrictions are lifted, we would not be comfortable traveling ... sigh. Virtual hugs from Viola the Birthday Person

Kathleen, a retired physician who is immune suppressed, wrote:

I plan to avoid community gatherings until I have vaccine on board for at least a month. That means I'll be in relative isolation for the long haul. Most Americans do not have immunity to this virus yet, and so much of the spread is from people who aren't having symptoms of illness. I believe there is huge potential for major resurgences.

Contemporary research on coronavirus is indicating that it may damage not only lungs but kidneys, hearts, and other parts of the body. It is not the flu. I'll be much better off with relative isolation than I would be with illness. I can't speak for Garrick. He is more of a risk-taker than I am, so if he indulges in social activity and trips, we may be keeping our distance from each other again.

After his travels at the start of the Covid, we self-quarantined in separate quarters, so we know the drill.

Pandemic Insights

Rolling Meadow was stringent in following CDC recommendations, regulations of both state and county, and Medicare guidelines. On a weekly schedule, our CEO coordinated with CEOs in other LPCs in our area, with officials in the local hospital, and with county and state officials.

Residents were strongly encouraged not to leave campus for reasons other than urgent medical, dental, or veterinary appointments. We could walk outside any time on our beautiful trails surrounding the complex. We could walk through the halls but were advised to "wear face masks, keep moving, don't stop for longer than a couple of minutes, and stay six feet apart." Visiting in anyone else's apartment was discouraged, and if we should *need* to enter someone else's apartment, everyone should be masked. To speak with a friend just two minutes' walk away, we phoned or texted, even next door.

Compliance was interesting. A few people reacted against restrictions: Frustrated, they would mutter, "This is America. I can do what I want" or "I agreed to Independent Living, not a prison." Others seemed confused. For example, they would wear a mask outdoors while walking alone but not inside while sitting in a circle of conversation, knowing that group gatherings were not even supposed to happen.

Some did not understand that a person could have the virus for several days with no symptoms but be highly contagious. Others did not comprehend that the virus could be aerosolized into tiny particles that might linger in the air, so that spending time indoors with others even amid small groups could be threatening, not even counting the health risks of mingling with other people off-property in stores or offices.

"It's very hard to imagine being contagious when you don't feel sick, especially in familiar situations, like when you're in your own home or with good friends. This is this virus's most deadly aspect: it is spreading before its carriers even know they have it. It's the termite of diseases – by the time you put your foot through the floorboard, it's too late."[43]

However, most residents cooperated with the guidelines and kept cheerful spirits. "At least we're safe here," they said, or "I miss seeing my friends, but I'm finding other things to do." Doing what? Cleaning closets, catching up on sleep, dipping paintbrushes into long unused watercolors, subscribing to new TV services, learning to use FaceTime and Zoom calls, and, while taking long walks on our beautiful campus, enjoying spontaneous short conversations with passers-by while standing six feet apart.

Early on, all employees were required to wear face masks. I applauded, for they set the standard, making masks reminders for us residents to wear ours. The clinic nurse said that, for non-medical people, the purpose of the mask was not just for protection but, more importantly, to remind individuals not to touch their faces. "All the time in the stores," she said, "I see people wearing gloves and masks: they touch the cart-handles and products, and then touch their faces. They don't realize how important it is to avoid touching your face." Because

---

[43] Luscombe, Belinda. "My Husband and I Knew the Dangers of the Coronavirus. How Could We Still Put Our Neighbor at Risk?" *Time*, July 20/July 27, 2020. p. 28.

finding a quantity of face masks was impossible, numerous residents and staff made hundreds of cotton masks using their own fabrics or bolts of colorfully printed material donated by local stores.

For the administration, an ongoing problem was the limited availability of Personal Protective Equipment (PPE) required by the staff. Across America, supplies were short, and items escalated fast in price. For example, given daily to all employees as they arrived for work, disposable face masks that used to cost five cents were now a dollar each. The prices of gowns and face shields were similarly inflated. At one point, our leadership was asking schools, dental offices, and agencies for donations of medical protective supplies. Finally, orders for PPEs began to arrive, still at highly inflated costs. Rolling Meadow continued to provide a safe environment.

In Independent Living, a few residents and staff became ill. Meanwhile, following CDC, state, and county guidelines, Covid tests were given routinely to all staff and employees in Assisted Living and in Skilled Nursing. Heightened attention focused on Skilled Nursing, where residents are the most vulnerable.

Early on, five residents in Skilled Nursing tested positive, and sadly two persons died. Eight staff tested positive; all went into quarantine at home, and all recovered and returned to work.

"Long-term care facilities are at the epicenter of the Covid epidemic in Pennsylvania and elsewhere. Those residents account for roughly 19% (19,225) of the 109,384 Pennsylvanians testing positive for the virus, and 68% of the 7,146 deaths, as of Tuesday [July 28, 2020). ...Public health experts contend that, without universal testing of residents and staff, early detection of asymptomatic individuals before they spread the illness is impossible."[44]

One section of the Skilled Nursing wing was cordoned off as a Covid unit. There, a dedicated staff of health care workers tended those who had tested positive, and in fact four of those workers moved from their own homes into a temporary apartment setting on Rolling Meadow property to quarantine in place with their patients.

As in other highly rated retirement communities, an Infection Control Nurse on the permanent staff helped everyone stay vigilant in preventing infection. Rolling Meadow established its Covid unit promptly and maintained it until all patients and all staff had tested negative for the preceding fourteen days. These medical efforts represented the thorough level of care that we residents were depending on.

To enforce a "no visitors" policy, barricades were erected across the two secondary entrances to the community, leaving one road open at the Main Entrance. There, a guard shack was set up and manned twelve hours daily to screen incoming and outgoing traffic. Containers of hand sanitizer appeared everywhere: in all common areas, at entrances, even within elevators. In the hallways, housecleaning staff sanitized everything that anyone could touch: varnished hand-railings, framed prints, tables, chairs.

To ensure less personal contact, workers went on twelve-hour shifts fewer days a week. Along with employees whose jobs were non-essential due to restrictions, the outside contractors who were installing an extensive new heating/air-conditioning system were

---

[44] Ciavaglia, Jo. "Nursing homes finish first round of testing," *The Intelligencer*. July 30, 2020. A1-2.

furloughed for nearly four months until the restrictions began to be lifted. Top to bottom, upper management to newest resident, preventing Coronavirus was the priority.

Don and I took these precautions seriously. We accepted that people with no symptoms could be carrying the virus and transmitting it to others, only to fall ill themselves a day or two later, and that WE could get it too. A physician on television advised that each person should behave as if he/she were sick and wants to protect others. Masks and social distancing were important to us. To hunker in our bunker was no hardship.

The kitchen stayed open, but the Dining Room was closed. For their own safety and ours, the teenage servers were furloughed. At first, Dining Services offered pick-up only, but when people were gathering in conversation at the pick-up point, the safer solution emerged: "We will deliver, please order at least a day ahead." The menu options were printed for one week at a time, one meal a day, and we could order the quantity we wanted. Residents in Assisted Living and in Skilled Nursing continued to receive three meals a day, delivered to their rooms. In Independent Living, where everyone has a full kitchen, providing one order a day worked well.

To supply our own kitchen, Don and I ordered online from the local grocery store, and our daughter Jane picked up the bags of groceries, bringing them to the main entrance where Don and I met her with a shopping cart. So popular was the grocery store's curbside delivery that customers had to start their orders a week ahead to receive (most of) the items seven days later. All in all, thanks to Dining Services delivery and curbside delivery, we ate well.

The local pharmacy offered free deliveries of prescriptions and necessities. We cancelled or postponed routine medical appointments for three months, and then used telehealth calls on computer, tablet, or smartphone for live, face-to-face checkups.

Communication among administration, staff, and residents was good. For example, we received frequent printed notices, and on in-house television, our CEO and our Executive Director gave weekly Administrative Updates. Just as in pre-pandemic days, our senior leadership team listened to residents, took their concerns seriously, and implemented procedures sensibly.

During the pandemic, residents stayed IN, visitors stayed OUT.

Being confined to quarters was not a problem. Don was usually at his computer in our office at one end of the apartment while I read, wrote, stitched, played music, or listened to podcasts in the living room. We met for lunch, practiced our partnership skills in bridge, went for a walk, and resumed whatever we were doing or started something else. After supper, we watched an hour of TV and then read.

I liked the slower pace very much. Having cancelled many activities, from theater to bridge dates to daytrips with others, I was surprised to become engrossed with in-home activities. We relaxed.

Enduring two years of Covid was scary. There were many unknowns about the virus itself. During the spring, summer, and fall, I took heart because Don and I could go outdoors every day, even on rainy days between showers. But I was concerned: What would we

208

do in the winter months when cold days and early darkness might require us to walk inside? Welcome was the decision that residents could walk but not congregate. Don and I could still walk one mile indoors, benefiting both the physical and the romantic heart.

What about breathing the air? With research demonstrating that aerosolized particles of Covid virus remain suspended in the air for hours, wearing masks was even more important in the winter. Our reality was that Don's and my only promise of safety would be the arrival of an effective vaccine that science laboratories across the whole world were speeding to create.

Amid the global Covid pandemic, I learned two new words that made me very glad to be living in Rolling Meadow: "*Immunoscenescence*: [the] natural tendency toward diminished immunity as we age; *Inflammaging*: [the] natural tendency toward more inflammation as we age, for Covid became recognized as a virus correlated with inflammation gone berserk. ... Aside from a deeply ingrained knowledge of handwashing and of just how far away 6 feet is, the Covid pandemic will, in the end, teach us more about our health vulnerabilities – individually and as an aging population."[45]

In 1955, my sister and I stood in line in a school gymnasium where five doctors sat at a long table injecting the newly created Salk polio vaccine into the arms of hundreds of children. The arrival of that vaccine ushered in a new era of protection against the dire consequences of polio. Amid the catastrophe of Covid, awaiting the development of the Covid vaccine, I figured that I would happily relinquish two years of socializing for ten more years of life.

---

[45] Zimmerman, Mike. "Who Gets Sick – and Why: An aging immune system can make you more vulnerable to disease. Covid-19 shows how important it is to keep yours strong," *AARP Bulletin/Real Possibilities*. May 2020. P.10,14.

12: Tales of the Pandemic

On December 10, 2020, the first Covid vaccine was given emergency approval, quickly followed by mass vaccinations. To date, we have had four boosters, and we will gladly continue them as recommended. Covid will always be with us, but thankfully its severity has been tamed.

During the lockdown, just for fun, I found myself writing limericks about our time of Covid. After a while, I had so many that I printed a booklet of them to sell as a money-raiser for our Benevolent Care fund here at Rolling Meadow. Chuckles added seasoning to the stew of everyday life in semi-quarantine:

Silly Rimes for Serious Times

We think Covid-19 is a menace.
We hate it with all that is in us.
  Though rules keep us safe,
  they sure make us chafe.
We'd rather be out playing tennis.

We yearn for release to be free
to visit the stores on a spree.
  The rules, they confine us –
  they're just a big minus.
May I please be the first vaccinee?

I find it is sad and unfair
That we can't put our trust in the air.
  With virus gone aerosol –
  a contagious, vast free-for-all –
Breathing air now requires great care.

I will walk on the path in the sun –
Spring's warm days have finally begun.
  Birds sing in the trees
  'neath gentle light breeze.
Spring's sights, sounds, and smells are such fun.

I see seniors now walking outside.
(At the Meadow, nobody can hide.)
  Some stop for a talk,
  some gaze at a hawk,
but we dare not drive out for a ride.

"We ought to be wearing a mask."
The Times recommended this task.
  It's easy to do,
  quite colorful too,
and hardly presumptuous to ask.

This Covid drags on like a dream:
stale sameness, pale palette, no gleam.
  Stuck staying at home,
  no safe place to roam.
Today I feel low, it would seem.

The restrictions are lightening up.
We drink freedom as if from a cup.
  We value our health
  as our most precious wealth.
We'll be cautious – we don't want to mess up.

We've been awfully good on our hill
while we swallowed this grim Covid pill.
  To ward off despair,
  we've trimmed our own hair
and grimaced a smile of good will.

211

After lots of cooperation,
our restrictions have reached a cessation.
If Covid comes back
in a Winter attack,
I'll consider those months a staycation.

Here's a billion-dollar idea ... a
smoke detector that shuts off
when you yell "I'm just cooking!"

Interlude 3: Stories of Life, Love, Loss

Creeper

With what stoic delicacy does
Virginia creeper let go:
the feeblest tug brings down
a sheaf of leaves kite-high,
as if to say, *To live is good*
but not to live – to be pulled down
with scarce a ripping sound,
still flourishing, still
stretching toward the sun –
is good also, all photosynthesis
***abandoned*, quite quits. Next spring**
the hairy rootlets left unpulled
snake out a leafy afterlife
up that same smooth-barked oak.
– John Updike[46]

The perpetual cycle of birth – life – death: these we celebrate, remember, ponder. Even when we don't want to think about death, we must face it when we lose people we know or love.

---

[46] Updike, John. From a ten-poem sequence "Endpoint" published posthumously, *The New Yorker*, March 16, 2009.

Fanny: I've just returned from two weeks in North Carolina visiting my friends. I lived there, right on the beach, for twenty years. I miss it a lot. I loved living there. I had so many friends and was always busy. I used to visit for a month at a time, but then people started dying and now I don't have as many friends there anymore.

Elaine: That presents a bittersweet situation, doesn't it, something I've realized since moving here. People die. Your friends die. And you can't dwell on that because you'd become depressed or gloomy. The challenge is to enjoy each person each day and focus on the good times.

Fanny: Yes, that's so. Don't think about the past, stay in the present and future. Make each day a good one.

I remember Carina, who used to walk the halls with her husband Thomas every day, chatting with passersby, greeting newcomers, sharing information, sometimes gossiping. Unexpectedly, Thomas fell ill and died within about two weeks. I think of others of our friends with whom we had dinners or conversations, and then they were gone. I notice how the spouses find ways to go on living. They grieve, they lower their heads, and they keep moving. I see them walking, visiting with others, resuming their activities.

It's comforting to think of a continuum of living. I compare it to a flowing stream that burbles along year after year. Sometimes at a curve, a tempest's torrents swirl out a portion of the bank, leaving a gash of newly exposed earth, but the storm subsides and as time passes, the wounded earth smooths, new foliage covers it, and the water resumes its passage.

Living in a retirement community confronts us with death more often than we may be used to, nudging us to think about when our own time comes, or our spouse's. These thoughts need not be gloomy, for indeed they sweeten the daily brew of life. "Look up, listen, see, appreciate, think, feel, enjoy it all this day."

For his protagonist in *Hamilton*, Lin Manuel Miranda pondered similar thoughts:

> **I imagine death so much it feels more like a memory**
> **When's it gonna get me?**
> **In my sleep? Seven feet ahead of me?**
> **If I see it comin' do I run or do I let it be?**
> **Is it like a beat without a melody?**
> **See, I never thought I'd live past twenty**
> **Where I come from some get half as many.**
> **Ask anybody why we livin' fast and we**
> **Laugh, reach for a flask,**
> **We have to make this moment last, that's plenty.**
> **– "My Shot," sung by Alexander Hamilton[47]**

Compassion: Bertha and Loss

Extending off the main corridor that curves through the Independent Living complex, our hallway was a cul-de-sac. In our little neighborhood, our relationships were especially close:

> I had to attend a funeral, and time was tight. In our hallway, however, I halted: Bertha was standing there, looking devastated, frozen. "Bertha, something's wrong! What's happening?" With a quaver, she said, "I just found out my sister died! I need to talk to someone!" Tears seeped down her cheeks. I hugged her and murmured comforting words, thinking I had to go but I couldn't leave her alone. "Just a minute," I said, "I'll get someone." I knocked on our neighbor's door: Maud energetically

---

[47] Miranda, Lin-Manuel & Jeremy McCarter. *Hamilton: The Revolution*. Hachette Book Group, Inc. 2016. 10.

opened it, and I drew close: "Bertha's in despair. Her sister died. She needs someone to talk to. Can you help her?"

Maud went to Bertha, embraced her, held her. They entered Bertha's apartment, and as I continued on my way to another person's "celebration of life," I knew that Maud was helping Bertha begin her own celebration of her sister's life.

Acceptance: Emmaline and Death

Emmaline had lingered two months with mysterious, alarming blood values. Just days before moving to Rolling Meadow a year before, she had endured a severe auto accident that resulted in constant pain. Emmaline's sudden decline had taken her first to the hospital and then to Skilled Nursing, with little hope of returning to her apartment to be with her husband of sixty years. Their daughter Rebecca posted updates on Walter and Emmaline's apartment door:

Thank you for the many prayers, cards, and voice mails offering support to Mom and Dad. We appreciate your care and concern. At this point, according to all Mom's doctors and specialists, there is nothing more to do for Mom. Her brain and body are shutting down. Some days are better than others. Some days she's able to carry on a conversation; some days she just wants to sit with her eyes closed and not be touched or spoken to. She might eat some of her meal, but an hour later, she won't be able to tell you what she ate. She might seem to enjoy a brief visit with someone, but an hour later, she won't be able to tell you who visited. Some days she might surprise us with a funny comment, and a few minutes later, she won't recognize the name of someone she's known for many years. ...

Our prayers for Mom have changed over the past weeks from "please heal Emmaline" to "if You're not going to heal her, please take her quickly, so she doesn't languish in pain and confusion." We encourage you to join us in praying for God to be merciful with her. Although His ways are not always our ways, we trust God and His sovereign plan.

[days later...]

It is with great joy but also sorrow that I tell you that Mom died last night. She finally saw Jesus face to face, and her faith was made sight. She is finally free from all pain and suffering. She is healed and enjoying the beginning of the rest of her life. ... We appreciate all your love and prayers. Thanks, too, for the love and friendship you all have given Mom through the years! She was well loved.

Death is a constant, wherever you live. Love is a constant too. Love beckons at any age, not just youth's hot passion but also elders' warm embers.

Forevermore: Lester's Young Love

Tall and slender with an aged cowboy's weather-tanned face, abundant white hair, plaid flannel shirt and blue jeans, Lester enlivened the dinner-table with his tale.

I grew up in Soda Springs in the southeast corner of Idaho just north of the Great Salt Lake. You could drink that carbonated water right out of the ground, and in fact it was bottled and sold. My dad was a farmer – barley and wheat but mostly barley. We were remote.

The town had a short Main Street lined with four or five bars. When my sister decided she was old enough to drive, she asked our dad for a ride to the town office. Once there, she announced, "I've come for a driver's license," so the clerk filled in a form, took a fee, and handed her the license. Being a thoughtful sort, and five feet ten inches tall, she went from bar to bar, shouted for attention, and said "I've just gotten my license and I've never driven before, so if you're parked along Main Street right now, just be warned that I'm gonna be tearin' down the center of town real soon." The bars emptied fast, and Main Street became an open highway for my sis.

I joined the Navy. They sent me to training camps in Oklahoma and Connecticut and then assigned me to the Naval Yards in Philadelphia, but the Yards were full, and they sent some of us across the river to Camden New Jersey where there was almost no work for us to do. A buddy and I were walking past the Y one evening when dance music drew our ears, and a sign lured us in: "All Servicemen Free." In we went.

After a while, I spotted a tall girl who looked pretty. "May I have the next dance?" I asked, and she said, "You can't do that dance." "What kind of a dance is it?" I said, and she answered, "A polka, and you don't look a bit Polish." "Well, don't tell ME what I can't do," I said, so she gave me her arm and off we went. When the music stopped, she said, "Where did you ever learn to polka like that?" I leveled with her: "Back in my town out West, my parents teach ballroom dancing." 'Guess she found a winner 'cause the two of us danced the whole evening.

I liked her, but I had only a dollar in my pocket. "Where do you live?" I asked. "Twenty-six blocks from here." "Can you walk it?" "That's how I got here." "May I walk you home?" The two of us set forth. Along the way, my dollar stretched for a couple of Cokes and a snack.

Twenty-six blocks is a long walk, but we finally arrived at her brick row-house that was at a corner. Just outside the front door was a bright streetlight, and she was awfully pretty. Well, I wanted to try to make out with her. Who wouldn't? I noticed next to her house an alley that extended into darkness. "Let's go along there," I pointed, and she said "Why?" "So, I can kiss you, o' course," I answered. She stepped back: "All you spent on me was a dollar, and for that you want some kissing too?" Well, that's how that evening ended, but I liked her a lot and kept on seeing her. We saw a future together.

The time came for her to meet my family in Idaho, but at the last minute I couldn't travel as scheduled. "I'll go on ahead," she offered, so my fearless New Jersey girl went alone by train all that way west to Idaho. She got on so well with my folks that I began to think they liked her more than me! We had nearly sixty years together.

Comfort: Carrie and Love at Life's End

In *Our Town*, Thornton Wilder wrote, "…people are meant to go through life two by two. 'Tain't natural to be lonesome." Psychologists find that couples report greater happiness and longer lives than singletons. Poets say love has no limits. Why should things be different in a retirement community?

Carrie smiles for everyone. She moves gracefully whether alone or when pushing a certain gentleman in a wheelchair. After I noticed that she lives alone in her apartment, curiosity compelled me to approach her: "I wonder whether I may ask you something. I notice that you and a gentleman often eat together and that you push him attentively in his wheelchair around the halls. May I ask whether he's your husband and does he perhaps live over in Assisted Living?"

Beaming her gracious smile, she replied, "No, we're not married. Erwin lived here with his wife before I came. I moved here

219

with my husband, and a few years later, he died. About the same time, his wife also died. It seemed natural for us to talk together and then to spend time together. We fell in love. We were both lonely, and it was wonderful to share that special feeling again. We had two splendid years together before he became ill. He moved to Assisted Living because he's permanently confined to a wheelchair, but we still spend as much time together as we can. We feel very fortunate to have this love between us."

Sharing: Rosaline and Unexpected Love

"Love" and "time together" are treasures in any setting.

I noticed that Rosaline, who lives alone, seems especially sharp. In our Stix class, where everyone slaps drumsticks in rhythm to music, she helps create a laugh-filled, festive sound. Alert to every detail, she speaks up to make sure everyone performs her and his best. Curious about her background, I expected her to be a retired teacher or nurse. I was wrong about that but right about asking for her love story:

I lived thirteen miles from here, but when my mother moved to Rolling Meadow, I used to visit her a lot and got to know many other residents. There was a couple my mother knew, close to her age. I liked them too. After the wife died, he took an interest in me. After some time passed, he told me he had decided to marry again, and he loved me, and he wanted to marry me. Would I marry him?

Well, what a surprise! I'd been a widow for years and hadn't really thought about marrying again. I said I couldn't marry him unless I loved him, and I didn't know whether I loved him or not. So, I went home and thought about him. After three days, I decided I did love him, and so we got married. I moved here to be

near him. That was about twenty years ago. We had ten good years together, and then he died. I've been here a long time, and my life has been good.

Birth, love, death. In our long lives, we experience them all. We make our way along the years as best we can.

Reflection

How soon we see the golden light
That leads our paths to peaceful rest at last –
The softened soothing glow that calms the mind
With memories lit within the hidden past.
Come soon my love my help my beauteous trust.
Join the journey fore and past
We too – we two can share the view:
The time, the feast, the joy of restful home.
                    – Janice Arrowsmith, 2011

I would be unstoppable if I could
just get started.

13: LPCs of The Future

Questions: How will Life Plan Communities evolve? What lifestyles will their twenty-first century residents have? Where will specialized LPCs be built? How will LPCs use their locations to promote healthy living? How will LPCs design their architecture for the future? How will new ideas in floor plans benefit residents? How will landscapes change? How will technology make community life easier, better, more fun?

In thirty years, about twenty percent of Americans will be over sixty-five. This huge group will use Medicare, require numerous health services, and need comfortable, safe places to reside. Senior living residential communities will be in demand across the country, not just in warm southern states but in seniors' former hometowns or near their adult children.

Expecting to have vigorous, stimulating lives, residents in senior living will want comfort, style, full service, and generous amenities. Needs for health services will expand as well, including care required when two residents live together into their nineties, even one-hundreds. Responding to these needs, Life Plan Community administrators are renovating and expanding existing properties; they also are envisioning new locations and innovative designs.

Some communities advertise their resort-like setting where everything is done for residents, who can simply relax and enjoy

223

themselves: "We'll take care of the cooking, cleaning, and yardwork, leaving you the time to enjoy your retirement."[48] However, the next wave of residents may want to be active with part-time and even full-time jobs, volunteer work, leadership roles, committee responsibilities, sports, hobbies, and anything else that they may be accustomed to do. Think of any retiree's oft-said phrase, "I'm so busy now that I don't know how I ever had time to work."

Contrasting twentieth to twenty-first century Life Plan Communities, Stephanie Aanenson writes, "Instead [of relaxation and luxury], design should support the kinds of lives people have always had, balanced with play, work, rest, and connection with others."[49]

"Location, Location, Location"

You learned these three essentials when you searched for your first house. Location is vital in retirement housing too. Life Plan Communities will be constructed in urban, suburban, and rural settings, in both well populated areas and remote "destination" sites.

Some LPCs will emphasize their smaller size: just two or three hundred residents. Others will promote their dramatic scenery: crashing ocean waves beneath grass-topped high cliffs, or startling red canyon walls dotted with gnarly trees, or stately mountaintops accessed by winding but safely constructed scenic roads. Some communities will offer specialized themes that suggest their resident profiles. For instance, an arts colony, an LBGTQ enclave, an international tract, a university of the mind.

---

[48] Newspaper insert. Hudson Estates Gracious Retirement Living, Hawthorn Senior Living, 2020. Received July 30, 2020.
[49] Aanenson, Stephanie. "Why Trendier Senior Living Amenities Might Not Be the Answer," www.seniorhousingnews.com. October 20, 2015, accessed June 6, 2020.

Other LPCs will feature neighborhood-style communal clusters each with a small, cozy feel because several apartments and suites surround a common entertainment/dining area and a shared garden-courtyard. Still others will include co-housing options. For instance, a "pack 'n go" offering encourages residents to stay six to twelve months in one retirement setting and then move on to another community so that vagabond explorers can experience their perfect lifestyle.

In summary, unique, dynamic locations will attract new retirees who yearn for something beyond what their parents had.

These examples sound high-end, intended for only the wealthy, but in fact expanding and new communities will strive to attract middle-class residents.[50] Partly financed by federal and state governments and already found across the country, subsidized low-cost housing features comfortable, safe apartments and houses that sometimes include health-care facilities. Often, because these affordable housing clusters are built as part of existing Life Plan Communities, they enjoy many LPC services and amenities as well.

At Rolling Meadow, when I asked the CEO how the plan to build affordable housing under the auspices of our community would affect my monthly fee, he replied, "It won't." I said, "If it would not cost or benefit us residents, why are you building it?" Straightforward, he answered, "Because the money is there to support it, we have a great need in our area to provide low-income housing, and we think it's the right thing to do." I realized that I may indeed

---

[50] Pew defines the middle class as those earning between two-thirds and double the median household income. This Pew classification means that the category of middle-income is made up of people making somewhere between $40,500 and $122,000. ("Which Income Class Are You?" *Investopedia*. November 20, 2019, accessed August 1, 2020.)

benefit by having new groups of people living in the area and, as a citizen, by participating in a program of social justice.

An LPC can intentionally use its site as part of its health and fitness appeal. For instance, in or near a large city, an LPC may advertise its "stimulating locale" that promotes walking for pleasure in or near cultural attractions including theaters, museums, restaurants of every level and taste, and parks, waterfronts, and urban trails. Farther from a big-town bustle, another community encourages walking to nearby libraries, local parks, cafés, shopping, and professional services. Even more distant from town centers, a community with expansive acreage designs the terrain with exercise-inviting features like meandering hiking trails, wide walkways, and scenic bicycle paths.

Interior Design for the Future

When you contract to move into an apartment or house in a Life Plan Community that is under construction or will be renovated to your specifications, your unit includes upgrades for tomorrow. You enjoy features that your previous home may not have had, especially if you lived there for decades. Moving at the end of a cold January from her house of fifty years, one friend said she especially loved a simple accessory that is standard now but new to her: a heat-fan in the bathroom ceiling.

Other upgrades include choices like a stackable washer/dryer, a warmth-giving electric fireplace, decorative moldings, granite countertops, and heated floors. Sometimes an option that was recently offered as a costly upgrade becomes standard just a year or two later because Marketing seeks always to attract new residents. An apt slogan in Sales may be, "We renovate to innovate, for the future is now."

However, offering just new or upgraded amenities will not be enough to attract future residents.[51] Other features of building design will be important. For example, think about the drab stairwells you've entered over the years in schools, colleges, hotels, and worksites. Built to code for emergency use, they may be cinderblocks painted in neutral tones with no or few windows, minimal signage, and no decoration. However, to promote daily wellness for all residents in retirement communities, redesign encourages walking between levels. Attractive wide stairwells include large windows, potted plants, interesting art, cheerful lighting, and upholstered benches at each landing. "Walking the stairs" becomes an enjoyable part of the day that also strengthens the heart and promotes well-being.

To welcome an abundance of natural light, common areas as well as apartments and houses have floor-to-ceiling glass walls and tall wide windows that draw the eyes outward and upward, uplifting the spirits. For the entire building, new designs feature spacious gathering rooms that combine services. For example, a pub/bistro/café area not only offers food and drink throughout the day and into the evening but also has shelves lined with books, magazines, board and card games, video-game cubicles, plus a computer study with PCs, printer, and fax. The display gallery in the Arts and Crafts wing may be surrounded by workshops for activities like metalcraft, woodwork, pottery and ceramics, fine arts, fabric crafts, theater arts, 3D printing, and robotics.

The Covid pandemic with its devastating effects on senior citizens stimulated engineers and architects to rethink health precautions for daily living in Life Plan Communities. For example, activity centers have open floor plans to suit frequent use in multiple ways:

---

[51] Aanenson, *ibid*.

easily cleaned moveable walls and furniture can accommodate movies, lectures, craft shows, dramatics, and spiritual services. Rolling plexiglass panels create socially distanced zones for safe gatherings in small groups.

In the Dining Room and other eating venues, including carry-out and delivery, each place setting includes an individually sealed soap towelette, and bowls of these small packets are placed at all other gathering spots. Throughout the building are attractive hand-washing stations and hand-sanitizer pumps. For cold and flu seasons, residents needing protection can swipe their electronic ID-cards at dispensers stocked with free face masks and tissue packets.[52]

In restrooms, many people dislike hot-air blowers that, while drying their hands, blast aerosolized, possibly germ-infested air to one and all. Into the future, virus-conscious restroom designers hang paper-towel dispensers near sinks and place trash receptacles next to the exit so that visitors can use their paper towels to touch door handles, then discard the paper as they depart.

Advances in heating and air conditioning include humidity control, for viruses thrive in dry air. Even more, going beyond just circulating heated or cooled air, new systems *ventilate* the air by bringing from the outside a constant flow of filtered fresh air. Just as contemporary hospital rooms exchange circulating air with fresh air six times an hour (and surgical theaters, twenty times an hour), residents inside their apartments and common areas have plenty of fresh air ventilation to maximize their respiratory health.

---

[52] In Japan, I noticed the waiters using tongs to place hot towels on little oval trays set before each diner. That hand-washing experience, in addition to other Japanese customs that ensure cleanliness, showed me how careless, even dirty, we Americans may seem to a hygiene-focused culture.

According to environmental engineer Linsey Marr, who studies how viruses and bacteria spread through the air, "Ventilation counts. [People should] Open windows and doors. Adjust dampers in air-conditioning and heating systems. Upgrade the filters in those systems. Add portable air cleaners or install germicidal ultraviolet technologies to remove or kill virus particles in the air."[53]

Altogether, the harrowing experiences with Covid produced permanent design advances that promote health in business, industrial, commercial, and residential buildings: enhanced hand hygiene, socially distanced common areas, and abundant fresh, clean, sanitized air.

Further, futurists have redrawn residential floor plans. For example, one group designing a project in a twelve-story Brooklyn building "updated the apartment schematics to reflect pandemic anxiety: the kitchen, the dining room, and the living room are all separable instead of flowing together; the bedrooms are spaced apart, for better acoustic buffering as workspaces, and include more square footage for desks; and the architects are aiming for thirty percent exterior space, with varied outdoor options. 'It's the importance of being able to get out, ... [to] be outside of the ecosystem for a little bit.'"[54]

In a recently constructed Life Plan Community, when you arrive at your new apartment or house, you step into the future. Truly,

---

[53] Marr, Linsey C. "Opinion: Yes, the Coronavirus Is in the Air - Transmission through aerosols matters - and probably a lot more than we've been able to prove yet," *The New York Times* online, July 30, 2020, accessed July 30, 2020.

[54] Chaka, Kyle. "Dept. Of Design-How the Coronavirus Will Reshape Architecture: What kinds of space are we willing to live and work in now?" *The New Yorker Today*. June 17, 2020. Accessed June 23, 2020.

your home is not only modern and comfortable but healthier than ever.

Landscaping for the Future

New construction, plus expansions and renovations in existing Communities, gives attention not just within the buildings but to the exterior as well. The grounds are filled with future-oriented changes.

Let's start with parking lots. Attending an Open House several years ago, I noted the enthusiasm of the Chief Executive Officer as she described the growth projected for her community, including new houses on the other side of a busy public road. She smiled:

> "Now, you're wondering where we'll put the parking lots and whether we will expand the ones we have. The surprise is that we will not be doing either option. For everyone, not just seniors, communities of the future will be less reliant on personal automobiles sooner than you may think. We will dial a number or click a link to order an electric car that will pick us up at our door, deliver us to our destination, and return to its garage to await the next call. We will return home the same way. The more people who use this service, the less it will cost. Meanwhile, car ownership, maintenance, insurance, and parking will become things of the past."

For our children, grandchildren, and us retirees living in Life Plan Communities, electric cars will take us to medical appointments, club meetings, shopping malls, and homes of friends and families. Becoming routine, this service will be easy, convenient, safe, and cost-effective. Not just parking lots but driveways and garages will be redesigned into useful, attractive home or landscape features.

For LPCs that have abundant acreage, traveling around the property will be convenient. At a call or click, robotic cabs will pick up passengers and take them to the fitness center, auditorium, dining hall, and game courts as well as to other residential clusters on property. A monorail looping around the campus will carry a cab that residents can summon by buzzing the callbox at each pickup point; a push on the "next stop" button will tell the cab at which mini station along its track the passengers want to be dropped off. Sheltered near residential clusters will be communal bicycles for exercise and adult tricycles equipped with baskets for shopping or picnics; residents will pedal not just to other buildings but along bike paths designed for exercise and scenic pleasure.

Attention will focus on landscaping more than just the grass, trees, shrubs, and flowerbeds. Created at the edge of the property will be a nature park whose sculpted hills feature trickling streams, outcroppings of rocks and boulders, walking paths with safe surfaces, nostalgic footbridges, and discretely placed handrails and lights. A pond and wildflower meadow will invite photographers, artists, walkers.

In this setting, wildlife will flourish with songbirds, butterflies, fish, ducks, cranes, migrating waterfowl, even groundhogs and foxes. Tucked into sheltered nooks will be benches inviting rest, reading, contemplation, picnicking, conversation, nature-study. Along the way will be a restroom with composting toilet and cold-water sink. Alone or with others, residents will be able to spend whole days outdoors.

Elsewhere on a vast campus will be an Outdoor Recreation area centered with benches, tables, water fountain, and another environmentally friendly restroom. Multi-use game courts will accommodate activities like bocce, pickleball, tennis, croquet, badminton, horseshoes, ring-toss, cornhole, Frisbee. Accessed by the same electronic key-fobs that residents use to enter their homes, the Activity Shed will store sets of game equipment along with scoreboards, rule books, and clipboards for schedules and rosters. Residents will play informally when they like or participate in scheduled group games.

Outdoor classes will include yoga, tai chi, and Zumba. At one end of the Outdoor Center, an enclosed dog-park will give pets a place to run, play, and socialize, with benches for owners to sit, relax, and visit. At the other end of the Center, a senior playground with adult-sized attractions will feature devices that make exercise fun. Traditional but adult-size tetherball, swings, and a maze will let residents relive youthful pleasures. Newly designed low-impact cardio equipment will be non-electric and non-computerized, just mechanical. People can work on balance and coordination while having fun outdoors. Just seeing these pictures makes you yearn to step up:

Top left, bottom left: Goric.com.

Bottom right: Lake Nockamixon State Park, PA.

Closer to the main building will be other inviting sites. The patio pub offers comfortable seating, a beverage bar, outdoor music, barbeques, firepits, space for dancing or trivia games, and a 16x16 foot black and white gameboard with eighteen-inch chess pieces or checkers. Waterfalls, trickling streams, and fish-ponds will nestle conversation nooks secluded near the meandering walking path that circles the entire community. A formal garden in one area will contrast with a casual English garden whose picnic grove invites BYO or catered meals outdoors. An amphitheater or in-the-round theater will invite outdoor performances, concerts, and movies.

Dotted around the property will be canopy swings, gazebos, a pavilion, and practical amenities like beverage stations and emergency callboxes. At cozy spots on rooftops, decks, and between buildings will be rock gardens, potted plants, self-contained waterfalls, and comfortable patio seating around small tables.

Will even one LPC contain all these features? Of course not. But will *your* community contain some of the outdoor attractions you would especially enjoy? Yes it will, because you will be looking for them!

Technology: The Future is Now

With three-fourths of people over sixty-five being online, older adults are tech-literate. At open-house Q&A sessions, someone always asks whether the community has Wi-Fi and how fast it is. Wanting to use their smartphones and laptops to continue their accustomed tech connections, residents seek excellent online access not just in their apartments and houses but throughout the buildings and the grounds outside. On their devices, they search the Internet, visit social media, communicate with friends, read books and magazines, play videogames, attend virtual meetings, talk person-to-person with distant family and friends, and view television and movies. A friend jokes, "You're not you without YouTube." I like to say, "My smartphone and I – perfect together!"

For seniors in care, so important is technology that the government makes donations to support them: "The State of Florida gave tablets to 150 nursing homes. The attorney general of Massachusetts supplied 750 tablets to nursing home residents. And Texas provided $3,000 per nursing home for tablets, webcams, and head-phones."[55]

For all residents in every state of health, telehealth usage soared during the Covid crisis. Medical professionals gave positive comments about virtual visits for routine calls and checkups. Even long-distance care increased. So popular and efficient were telehealth appointments that many providers continued their use after the pandemic ended.

In Life Plan Communities, advances in technology are already creating an exciting new normal: Electronic locks and video-monitoring improve building and grounds security. Residents can wear monitors that contain lightweight chips so small they can be in a finger-ring, a skin patch, or even an insert under the skin. Already widely used are wearable devices that sense movement, heart rate, temperature, impact from a fall, or immobility. Detection of any abnormal event triggers a computerized alert that notifies the staff of irregularities. The staff can then call for emergency help to be sent to the resident's exact location, along with an electronic display of that person's health records.

The campus of the future will have features that already have begun. It will be cashless because residents will make all transactions with their electronic key-fobs. Within apartments and houses, wall-mounted video touchscreens will display an array of community news, events, and activities. Residents will use on-screen touch options to register for programs, order food, submit work-orders, and seek information; they can schedule time in the pool, wellness class, or Outdoor Center; they can make clinic appointments and dining reservations, explore the photo gallery, access the resident/staff

---

[55] Aging and Health Technology Watch: Industry Market Trends, Research & Analysis, https://www.ageinplacetech.com/. Accessed June 13, 2020.

Directory, roam the library listings, and ask questions. If a resident is disabled, voice-recognition technology will allow touchless access to all these features. "Randy the Robot" will deliver mail, small packages, and snacks while its watchful electronic camera-eye will monitor the hallways for neatness and irregularities like burned-out light bulbs.

On residents' TV screens and computer monitors, Communities broadcast meetings, classes, lectures, games, social events, church services, training sessions, senior-focused video games, and exercise classes.[56] Imagine! During the Pandemic, residents at Rolling Meadow tasted the effectiveness of virtual meetings and found them entirely palatable. Yes, their offering could be improved, but as the Disney Imagineers say, if you can envision something, it can happen. Can you imagine virtual meetings that are livelier, more immediate? ...enhanced with live links that expand what the speaker is saying or doing? ...interactive from participants' home-screens? These and more innovations will appear as users articulate what they want or need.

Think of the places you can go, the things you can do, from the comfort and safety of your own home. Residents who are housebound or physically fragile can participate in activities and events, visit family and friends, and enjoy arts and entertainment far beyond what their physical limitations might have allowed. In fact, in the Artificial Reality Studio, they can wear virtual reality (VR) headsets to travel the land, sea, and universe, in the past/present/future, real or fantasy, in the comfort of a cushioned recliner.

All residents will benefit from the stimulation of high-tech activities: their brains will be active, and they will feel included in what

---

[56] Breeding, Brad. "The CCRC of the Future: Technology," www.mylifesite.net. September 30, 2019, accessed June 6, 2020.

they enjoy doing. In fact, eager personalities risk being overwhelmed by so much wonderment, for they must choose just a few delicious morsels from a fabulous smorgasbord of high-tech offerings.

Just as now, seniors of the future want Life Plan Communities that offer style, service, amenities, exercise choices, dining variety, and entertainment at a level equal to or better than they enjoyed when they made the decision to move. They know that physical and social activity prolong life, that staying active is part of staying healthy.

Many features of the future are available right now, and others are on the way. Some cost more money, such as outdoor dining or tennis courts that may be found at luxurious communities; others require just the vision and desire to be adopted into the budget, such as cozy enclaves along a walking path or computer/monitor desks located at gathering places.

These future-oriented elements drive management and market-ing in their common effort to attract new residents. For residents at every level of health – perfectly fit, somewhat disabled, house-bound, forgetful – advances in technology stimulate cognitive skills, expand horizons, and promote emotional well-being.

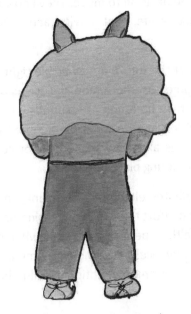

I burn about 2000 calories every time I put fitted sheets on the bed by myself.

Conclusion

Questions: Why may living in a Life Plan Community be the best option for me?

Goals: Dignity. Choice. Independence. Friends. Having served our families, careers, and country, we can now serve ourselves by setting priorities to provide secure living for the rest of our lives.

Who can predict the future? The best we can do is to try to prepare for whatever may happen. For example, after seven years in Rolling Meadow, our hall neighbors Esther and Travis had to move to Assisted Living because they had declined physically and mentally. Don and I were glad they could have the help and safety they needed in their new home. Meanwhile, many other friends their age were doing well indeed in Independent Living. At 91, Sabina leads a team of residents who fill orders for fresh produce every Friday morning; at 100, Jacob works on 1000 piece puzzles every day while enthusing about last night's football or baseball game; at 102, Ramona drives every Monday to play duplicate bridge.

As time moves along, we would all like to be sturdy, robust, vigorous; but the fact is that we just do not know how the years will affect us.

Observing fellow residents has affirmed what I had concluded during the search for our retirement community: the best time to move to a Life Plan Community is when we are energetic, healthy, and enthusiastic. That way, as the calendar moves along, we know we will be in a comfortable, safe setting no matter our state of health.

We who move to a retirement community can look forward to enjoying living for the rest of our senior years.

Deciding to move from a beloved home is hard.

Exploring all the options is daunting.

Feeling confident about the future may be difficult.

Even so, I urge seniors to think ahead, to set priorities, and then to pursue them, now.

The past is gone. The present is a gift.

You have one life. And it's right now. In front of you. So GO!

Illustrations

"Bunnies" by Marilyn Deatelhauser

pen 'n ink with watercolor

Beatrice Bunnet ("She's French, you know") and her long-eared friends came to life in 2020 when Marilyn saw a cartoon and thought, "I could do that!" In 2012, after she had retired, she began painting in watercolors and making her own note cards. Every few weeks, Marilyn posts a new bunny on her hallway bulletin board. In 2023, she exhibited her collection in the art gallery near the arts and crafts room in her own Life Plan Community.

I'm off to the Creative Arts Studio
to paint. So much fun! Why
don't you try it sometime?

I'm giving up eating chocolate for
a month. Sorry, bad
punctuation. I'm giving up.
Eating chocolate for a month.

Helpful Sources on the Internet

Continuing Care/Life Plan Communities

My LifeSite:

https://www.mylifesite.net/ – "... the most thoroughly researched CCRC information on the web. ... a great way to research senior living. ... We provide detailed, objective information and tools for consumers and their advisors." You can register for and have free or paid access to search and compare some communities, explore a resource library, preview a financial calculator.

National Continuing Care Residents Association:

https://www.naccra.com/ – "We collaborate nationwide with residents and prospective residents of Continuing Care Retirement/Life Plan Communities and allied organizations for the purpose of promoting, protecting, and improving the CCRC/Life Plan lifestyle. We help current residents monitor the ongoing health and performance of the community where they now live and supply valuable tools and services." Membership fee: $25/household.

LPCs as Businesses

American Seniors Housing Association:

https://www.seniorshousing.org/ – "Created in 1991, ASHA represents the interests of more than 500 companies involved in the finance, development, and operation of the full spectrum of housing and services for seniors – including independent living, assisted living, memory care, and continuing care (or life plan) communities. ASHA primarily focuses on legislative and regulatory advocacy, research, and educational opportunities and networking for senior living executives."

Commission on Accreditation of Rehabilitation Facilities (CARF):
https://carf.org – "… an independent, nonprofit accreditor of health and human services [whose] mission is to promote the quality, value, and optimal outcomes of services through a consultative accreditation process and continuous improvement services that center on enhancing the lives of persons served."

Leading Age:
https://leadingage.org/ – "The trusted voice for aging. … LeadingAge's policy approach begins with providers – thousands of people working at life plan communities, assisted living, memory care, nursing homes, adult day centers, home care and hospice agencies, and other settings on the front lines of care and services." Resource for employees and management of life plan communities.

Over-55 and Senior Co-op Housing

Senior Cooperative Housing:
http://seniorcoopliving.org/ – "Senior cooperative housing provides vibrant, affordable living with a neighborly perspective for active adults 55+. Owned and controlled by the members themselves, cooperatives are not-for-profit organizations that are uniquely intentional about creating well-designed, socially supportive communities. Cooperatives preserve members' financial resources and enhance their lives." (Minnesota-based)

Remaining in Your Own Home

Naturally Occurring Retirement Community (NORC):
https://aging.ny.gov/naturally-occurring-retirement-community-norc – "Classic and neighborhood NORCs, collectively known as the NORC program, coordinate a broad range of health and social services to help support older

residents age in their own homes, as well as utilize the strength of the older residents in the design, implementation, and prioritization of services and activities. The intent of the NORC program is to facilitate and integrate the health and social services already available in the community, as well as organize those necessary to help meet the goal of enabling older adults to remain at home." (New York State Office for the Aging)

Caregiving at Home

AARP Resources – Family Caregiving:
https://www.aarp.org/caregiving/ – Links include Care at Home, Nursing Homes, Medical, Financial & Legal, Life Balance, Community, Local Resources & Solutions.

Family Caregiver Alliance:
https://www.caregiver.org/ – "Coalition of organizations focused on family caregiving issues. Conducts research, policy analysis and develops national programs to increase public awareness of family caregiving issues."

Friends Life Care:
https://www.friendslifecare.org/ – "Enjoy your retirement years with an affordable plan that protects your savings and health so you can remain independent at home as you age. ... Aging in Place: If you'd prefer to stay in your home as you age, there are steps you can take today to protect your lifestyle, your loved ones, and your finances tomorrow. So, no matter what changes, what's most important to you is secure."

Home Instead Senior Care:
https://www.homeinstead.com/ – Home Instead Senior Care® understands that our most vulnerable populations need help now more than ever. If you have an aging loved one who needs care, we can help. ... We put relationships and safety first to help older adults remain in their own homes.

Long-Term Care Insurance

American Association for Long-Term Care Insurance:
https://www.aaltci.org/ – "Find the most current information including long term care insurance costs, ways to save, tax deductibility rules and long-term insurance companies and their ratings."

Financial Information for Seniors

Genworth (Insights about Costs/Paying for Care):
https://www.genworth.com/ – "... we have been focused on helping our customers navigate caregiving options, protect, and grow their retirement income, and prepare for the financial challenges that come as we age. We're here to be a trusted ally for everybody who needs care as they age and anybody who loves them."

Grandfolk:
https://grandfolk.com/ – "There's no need to purchase on a hunch. ... financial services, shopping products and care services ... quantitative and qualitative assessments of product features..."

Senior Living Financial Resources:
https://www.seniorliving.org/ – "... our experts search high and low for the best resources to ... provide in-depth research, rankings and reviews." Find deals, give comparisons and suggestions on such topics as senior housing, personal finance, insurance, health products, transportation, and mobility issues.

Help for Veterans

U.S. Department of Veterans Affairs:
https://www.usa.gov/federal-agencies/u-s-department-of-veterans-affairs "The Department of Veterans Affairs runs programs benefiting veterans and members of their families. It

offers education opportunities and rehabilitation services and provides compensation payments for disabilities or death related to military service, home loan guaranties, pensions, burials, and health care that includes the services of nursing homes, clinics, and medical centers." Links include benefits, social security questions, affordable rental housing, and partnership programs for Long Term Care Insurance.

Help from Your State

To find **your state's Department of Aging**, Google the name of your state + "department of aging."

Help from Medicare and Medicaid

https://www.medicare.gov/
"A federal government website managed and paid for by the U.S. Centers for Medicare & Medicaid Services."

https://www.healthcare.gov/
Get coverage; Keep or Update your plan.

https://www.mymedicare.gov/
Create an account for a more personalized experience.

https://www.medicaid.gov/
Medicaid: Federal Policy Guidance, State Overviews, Basic Health Program. "Every state's Medicaid program is changing and improving – most states are expanding coverage for low-income adults..."

https://www.cms.gov/
Centers for Medicare & Medicaid Services: Medicare, Medicaid, Medicare-Medicaid Coordination, Private Insurance, Regulations & Guidance, Research & Statistics

https://www.hhs.gov/
U.S. Department of Health and Human Services: Public Health, Human Services, Healthcare

Life Expectancy Calculator

How long do the actuaries think you may live?
https://www.ssa.gov/OACT/population/longevity.html

Making plans sounds like fun
until you have to put clothes on
and actually go out.

Bibliography

Adamson, Dr. Glenn. "A Retirement Home's Lessons in How to Keep in Touch: A curator finds much to admire in the creative exuberance of the objects in these halls," *The New York Times*. September 22, 2018.

"ADL/IADL Checklist," https://www.seniorplanningservices.com/files/2013/12/Santa-Barbara-ADL-IADL-Checklist.pdf accessed June 18, 2020.

"Adult Playgrounds and You," www.goric.com. Accessed June 6, 2020.

Aging and Health Technology Watch: Industry Market Trends, Research & Analysis, https://www.ageinplacetech.com/. Accessed June 13, 2020.

"American Generation Fast Facts," CNN Library. CNN.com, updated August 17, 2019. Accessed June 2, 2020.

"Antonio Carluccio: My Life in Five Dishes," BBC News: World Service. www.bbc.co.uk. Accessed June 2020.

"Goals for Safe Driving (... and for Life!)," Introduction, Unit 6, "Goals of the Course," AARP Safe Driving video instructional course. Accessed January 2020.

"Heading Into Retirement During A Down Market: A conservative withdrawal approach is part of a sustainable retirement spending plan." *T. Rowe Price Investor*. Summer 2020. 6-9.

"My LifeSite," www.myLifeSite.net. Accessed June 16, 2020.

Aanenson, Stephanie. "Why Trendier Senior Living Amenities Might Not Be the Answer," www.seniorhousingnews.com. October 20, 2015, accessed June 6, 2020.

AARP Caregiving Resource Center. www.aarp.org/home-family/caregiving/.

Bibliography

Age in Place. www.AgeInPlaceTech.com. Aging & Health Technology Watch: Industry trends.

American Association of Long-Term Care Insurance. www.aaltci.org.

"Ask the Doctors: Loneliness linked to a number of diseases, conditions," *The Intelligencer*. Gannett/Doylestown PA. July 15, 2020, C7.

Baker, Melinda. "Cover Story – Audiobook Month: The Power of Performance," *BookPage*, June 2020. 10.

Breeding, Brad. "4 Ways to Know You're Ready to Consider a CCRC Move," blog. February 10, 2020, accessed June 16, 2020.

Breeding, Brad. "Aging in Place: Hidden Costs of Using Family as Caregivers," mylifesite.net. May 27, 2015, accessed June 6, 2020.

Breeding, Brad. "Can I Use My Long-Term Care Insurance in a CCRC?" https://www.mylifesite.net/blog/post/can-i-use-long-term-care-insurance-in-CCRC/ December 16, 2019, accessed June 16, 2020.

Breeding, Brad. "CCRCs Need to Solve the 'Not Ready Yet' Demographic Issue," blog. June 22, 2020, accessed June 24, 2020.

Breeding, Brad. "How Does Nursing Home Billing Work?" Mylifesite.net. June 3, 2016, accessed June 5, 2020.

Breeding, Brad. "How Senior Living is Evolving to Meet Future Demand," https://www.mylifesite.net/blog/post/how-senior-living-is-evolving-to-meet-future-demand/ June 1, 2020, accessed June 6, 2020.

Bibliography

Breeding, Brad. "The CCRC of the Future: Community Design," www.mylifesite.net. September 23, 2019, accessed June 4, 2020.

Breeding, Brad. "The CCRC of the Future: Technology," www.mylifesite.net. September 30, 2019, accessed June 6, 2020.

Breeding, Brad. "The Great Debate: Rental or Entry Fee Retirement Community?" https://www.mylifesite.net/blog/post/rental-or-entry-fee-retirement-community/ May 25, 2020, accessed June 16, 2020.

Chaka, Kyle. "Dept. Of Design – How the Coronavirus Will Reshape Architecture: What kinds of space are we willing to live and work in now?" *The New Yorker Today.* June 17, 2020, accessed June 23, 2020.

Ciavaglia, Jo. "Nursing homes finish first round of testing," *The Intelligencer.* July 30, 2020. A1-2.

CNN Library. "American Generation fast Facts," CNN.com. Updated August 17, 2019, accessed June 2, 2020.

Cura Hospitality. www.CuraHospitality.com. Accessed June 3, 2020.

Eaton, Joe. "Special Report, The New Normal: Your Health – Reimagining the Nursing Home: After Covid, here's what experts say may change," *AARP Bulletin Real Possibilities.* June 2020. 16-18.

Elder Web. www.elderweb.com.

Elinor North America www.elior-an.com. Accessed June 3, 2020.

Esswein, Patricia Mertz & Sandra Block. "Retire in Style at a Continuing Care Retirement Center," *Kiplinger's Personal Finance.* September 2014. Kiplinger.com, accessed June 2, 2020.

Bibliography

Feldman, Nina & Laura Benshoff. "Nursing homes as we know them are over: Covid fuels push to home-based care," https://whyy.org/articles/nursing-homes-as-we-know-them-are-over-covid-19-fuels-push-to-home-based-care/ June 12, 2020, accessed June 14, 2020.

Fingersh, Julie. "When Older Relatives Shrug at Coronavirus Restrictions," *New York Times Online*, April 15, 2020.

Frederick Living Continuing Care Retirement Community, https://frederickliving.org/about-us/core-values-mission/ accessed July 17, 2020

Friedman, Sally. "New home, new beginning," *The Intelligencer*. February 9, 2020, B3.

Friends Life Care. https://www.friendslifecare.org

Fry, Richard. "The pace of Boomer retirements has accelerated in the past year," Nov. 9, 2020. https://www.pewresearch.org/fact-tank/2020/11/09/the-pace-of-boomer-retirements-has-accelerated-in-the-past-year/. Accessed December 2, 2020.

Genworth Financial Cost of Care Study 2013: www.genworth.com/corporate/about-genworth/industry-expertise/cost-of-care.html.

Gomez, Alan. "Humans 'are not meant to be alone': Loneliness can lead to mental, physical decline," Nation's Health, *USA Today*. May 26, 2020. 1D.

Harrigan, John E., Jennifer M. Raiser, Phillip H. Raiser. *Senior Residences: Designing Retirement Communities for the Future*. John Wiley & Sons, Inc., NY. 1998.

Bibliography

Hedges, Michael, interviewer. "Q&A Deborah Birx, M.D.: 'If People Do Get Reexposed, They Will Make Antibodies Very Quickly," *AARP Bulletin Real Possibilities*. June 2020. 4.

Hockman, David. "Cover Story, Special Report, The New Normal: What Comes Next – Experts Predict How the Pandemic Will Change Our Lives," *AARP Bulletin Real Possibilities*. June 2020. 10-12.

Home Instead Senior Care. www.HomeInstead.com.

Huxhold, John. "The Mail," *The New Yorker*. December 30, 2019.

Jenkins, Jo Ann, CEO. "Your AARP, Special Report, The New Normal – Fighting for You: Today and Tomorrow – We're prepared to take on the changes needed for a better future," *AARP Bulletin Real Possibilities*. June 2020. 36-37.

Jukes, Helen. "Behind the Book: Making a Home Among the Bees," *BookPage*. May 2020. 14, 15.

"Kodak Misses Its Moment" in Spectacular Failures, podcast, Stitcher, accessed July 24, 2019.

Kondo, Marie. *the life-changing magic of tidying up: the Japanese art of decluttering and organizing*. Ten Speed Press, 2014, 42.

Krystal, Arthur. "'Old News: Why can't we tell the truth about aging?' A Critic at Large," *The New Yorker*, November 4, 2019, 77.

Leading Age Support Center. www.ltsscenter.org.

Leading Age. www.LeadingAge.com. Accessed March 4, 2020.

Leisure Care. https://www.leisurecare.com/resources/continuing-care-communities-vs-life-plan-communities/, accessed May 25, 2020.

Bibliography

Lender, Jeanne. "Special Report, The New Normal: Your Health –
The Future of Health Care is Here: The pandemic has turned
telehealth from a 'maybe, one day' to a 'right here, right now.'"
AARP Bulletin Real Possibilities. June 2020. 21-24.

Luscombe, Belinda. "My Husband and I Knew the Dangers of the
Coronavirus. How Could We Still Put Our Neighbor at Risk?"
Time, July 20/July 27, 2020. p. 28.

Marr, Linsey C. "Opinion: Yes, the Coronavirus Is in the Air –
Transmission through aerosols matters – and probably a lot
more than we've been able to prove yet," *The New York Times
Online*, July 30, 2020, accessed July 30, 2020.

Medicare. www.medicare.gov.

Miranda, Lin-Manuel & Jeremy McCarter. *Hamilton: The
Revolution*. Hachette Book Group, Inc. 2016. 10.

Moss, Rebecca. "Care Homes: The virus exploited problems state
had failed to address," *Philadelphia Inquirer*. June 14, 2020. A1.

My Life Site, mylifesite.net, Osterholm, Michael. "Steady Voice in a
Storm," *USA Today*, May 5, 2020, A1.

National Alliance for Caregiving. www.caregiving.org/resources.

Naturally Occurring Retirement Communities. www.norcs.org.

Osterholm, Michael. "Steady Voice in a Storm," *USA Today*, May 5,
2020, A1.

PACE. www.medicare.gov/your-Medicare-costs/help-paying-
costs/pace/pace.html.

Phoebe ww.phoebe.org.

Rubin, Gretchen. *The Four Tendencies: The Indispensable
Personality Profiles That Reveal How to Make Your Life Better*

(and Other People's Lives Better, Too). Harmony Books/Penguin Random House LLC: NY. 2017.

Senior Coop Housing. www.senior coopliving.org.

Shaw, Jim. "How to Minimize Food Waste in Commercial Kitchens: Try these tips to cut unnecessary expenses and help the environment," FSR. April 2017. https://www.fsrmagazine.com/expert-takes/how-minimize-food-waste-commercial-kitchens, accessed July 12, 2020.

TFG Wealth Management, print media advertisement slogan. February 2020.

Tobenkin, David. "Choosing a Retirement Community," *NARFE*. May 2020, 24-30.

Updike, John. From a ten-poem sequence "Endpoint" published posthumously, *The New Yorker*, March 16, 2009.

U.S. Department of Veterans Affairs.

Wang, Penelope. "Can Your Retirement Be Saved?" *Consumer Reports*. July 2020. 44-47.

Waverly Heights. www.WaverlyHeightsltd.org. Accessed June 4, 2020.

"Which Income Class Are You?" Investopedia. November 20, 2019, accessed August 1, 2020.

Zimmerman, Mike. "Who Gets Sick – and Why: An aging immune system can make you more vulnerable to disease. Covid shows how important it is to keep yours strong," *AARP Bulletin Real Possibilities*. May 2020. P.10-14.

Winter: The next time I hear
"salt and ice," it better be a
margarita recipe.